PRAISE FOR
Created for the Impossible

In her book *Created for the Impossible*, Krissy Nelson draws her readers into a deeper understanding of their relationship with God. She uses her own beautiful testimonies and the Word of God to demonstrate what our lives can look like when we "dare to dream" with God and know who we are in Him. As you read this book, I pray that you will know the profound love God has for you and the huge destiny over your life. You really are created for the impossible.

HEIDI G. BAKER, PHD
Co-Founder and CEO of Iris Global
author of *Birthing the Miraculous*

Created for the Impossible is a book birthed out of Krissy Nelson's genuine, prophetic, destiny-defining encounters with God—and the wonderful thing is, these encounters are not exclusive to the author. Krissy presents her personal experiences as unique invitations for you to meet God in the same ways. Sure, the unfolding of your story will be different than hers. It should be! However, I encourage you to pay close attention to the powerful, prophetic words that Krissy shares out of her own history with God—one of those might very well be a conduit that connects you with the voice of the Lord, summoning you into unexplored, uncharted territories of living beyond the confines of anything you could hope, dream or imagine. And yet, doesn't that sound like the Lord?

As publisher of Destiny Image, this is one of those unique books that captures the DNA of what founding publisher and prophet, Don Nori Sr., envisioned when he received the mandate to publish the prophets. Krissy would not classify herself as a prophet, but her book contains a relatable, yet prophetic edge that—I promise—will release a glorious divine discontentment over you. Discontentment for "normal" living. Discontentment for just going through the everyday motions. Discontentment with waiting for some big break before you step out and walk in the assignment of the Lord for your life. Reading *Created for the Impossible* releases a life over you that awakens dead and dormant areas to new God-possibilities right where you are!

This is no static endorsement. I highly commend both the message *and* the messenger to you! I have ministered alongside Krissy Nelson and have seen her heart for God in action. She's the real deal.

As you get ready to dive in, remember: when you discover that you were born to challenge the impossibilities of life, small thinking and small living go out the door and you will find yourself running into the wide-open Kingdom-advancing, mountain-taking, territory-conquering life that Jesus made available for you!

LARRY SPARKS
Publisher, Destiny Image
Author of *Breakthrough Faith*, compiler of *Ask for the Rain*,
and co-author of *The Fire That Never Sleeps*

In *Created for the Impossible*, my friend Krissy Nelson uncovers the unfathomably awesome truths about what God believes about you. Then, in her usual winsome, graceful way, she explores how to partner with Him to break out of the box of small thinking...to dream impossible dreams...to fearlessly follow Him into more than you could ever hope or imagine. Get ready to join Krissy on a spellbinding journey to finally experience the adventure God designed for you!

KYLE WINKLER
Author of *Activating the Power of God's Word*
and creator of the Shut Up, Devil! App
www.kylewinkler.org

I am certain that Joseph struggled to hold on to his God-given dreams while in slavery and prison. All dreamers have to learn how to nurture their dreams until those dreams come into fruition. Krissy Nelson's book, *Created for the Impossible*, will inspire you to dream again as you see God's hand actively involved in the tapestry of your daily life. Everyone needs to dream and every dreamer needs to read this book.

RICHARD CRISCO
Lead Pastor, Rochester Christian Church
Rochester, Michigan

Without vision we perish. If there is a flicker of hope or embers of a dream, allow the words in this book to breath upon them and by the grace of God dare to do the impossible with Him. Krissy Nelson pulls faith from within you and draws you to posture yourself to do what only God can conceive.

MARY WELLS
Co-Founder, His Reward Ministries
www.hisreward.org

Reading Krissy's book is like taking a walk with a good friend. You realize that as Krissy continues to speak, the path you share reflects her journey. One step at a time you are led to a beautiful vista where you can see yourself as God sees you. Read this book and be uplifted!

PASTORS BOB AND SHARON ONA
First Assembly
Fargo, North Dakota

I found Krissy Nelson's book an intriguing read. Once started it was hard to put down. I appreciated not only her transparency and the story of her journey, I also found her insights into the Lord's leading and guiding us very helpful and useful in everyday living. It's a very practical book along with good life principles! A must read for all of us on the journey to get closer to the Lord.

DR. EVON G. HORTON
Senior Pastor, Brownsville Assembly
Pensacola, Florida

I've seen many books and heard numerous sermons on "Identity," but Krissy Nelson's *Created for the Impossible* stands out above them all. Through her own down-to-earth stories, showered with lessons learned from her own life and her children, she led me to a deeper faith and a fresh perspective on identity in Christ. This is Krissy's genuine, heartfelt, true-life story of how she walked out of pain and discouragement into a life which exudes with contagious joy. Her life shines brightly with the love and light of Jesus, and this book will inspire your heart to shine as well.

What I love the most is that every chapter is anchored in the centrality of the cross and sprinkled with the blood of the Lamb. As you read these pages, you will see that your story has been woven into His-story with a beautiful crimson thread. You will indeed discover that it's OK to color outside the lines, and when you open the shining gift God has for you, as Krissy says, the breath of God will release over you and the Holy Spirit will burst inside you as a flame of fire. Then the Spirit of God will help you see the intense sparkle of compassion and love in Jesus' eyes. Lock eyes with Him and soon your confidence in Him will soar and your life will reflect the radiant light of Christ to a world desperate for hope.

SANDY DAVIS KIRK, PhD
Author, Founder of Camp America Ablaze, Inc.
and Behold Ministries, www.behold-ministries.org

Created for the Impossible

Created for the Impossible

BREAK EVERY HINDERING THOUGHT, BELIEVE WHAT GOD SAYS ABOUT YOU

KRISSY NELSON

DESTINY IMAGE® PUBLISHERS, INC.

P.O. Box 310, Shippensburg, PA 17257-0310

"Promoting Inspired Lives."

This book and all other Destiny Image and Destiny Image Fiction books are available at Christian bookstores and distributors worldwide.

Cover design by Eileen Rockwell

Interior design by Terry Clifton

For more information on foreign distributors, call 717-532-3040.

Reach us on the Internet: www.destinyimage.com.

ISBN 13 TP: 978-0-7684-1170-6
ISBN 13 eBook: 978-0-7684-1171-3
ISBN 13 HC: 978-0-7684-1542-1
ISBN 13 LP: 978-0-7684-1543-8

For Worldwide Distribution, Printed in the U.S.A.

1 2 3 4 5 6 7 8 / 21 20 19 18 17

DEDICATION

This book is dedicated to my amazing, handsome, godly husband, Donovan, your love, support, and prayers launched me into this wild adventure of the unknown. Seeing dream after dream fulfilled by God was in large part due to your faithful prayers, your unyielding love for me, and your sacrifice! I thank God for you, my love. He made you knowing that you are the perfect fit for me. I couldn't follow the dreams of my heart as I do, if it weren't for you. You challenge me, you love me, and you help fan into flame the fire inside me to press on toward the goal to win the prize for which God has called me heavenward in Christ Jesus (see Phil. 3:14).

To my daughter Jenessa, as I've said before, you brought Mommy back to life again! The dreams of my heart had nearly died. They were up on a shelf, pushed to the back, covered in dust...and then you came along, and your life brought life surging back through my veins! God used you to remind Mommy that anything is possible. Through that tenacious sparkle in your eye and that whimsical, yet courageous heart of yours, you inspired so much of this book and the revelation that God loves us just as we are, that we don't need to bring anything to the table to impress Him, that He's proud of us simply because we're His child. I love you my sweet pumpkin pie...you have my heart, and you know you have God's heart too.

To my son Justice, your life brought me to a whole new level of faith and trust in the Lord. Before you were even born, your mommy and daddy prayed over you and boldly and courageously believed for your wholeness and well-being. We stood on the vision God gave us for our son and were uncompromising in prayer! Your birth proved the miraculous handiwork of God. Today you pray with such a prophetic voice, your compassion for others encourages me to flow in greater compassion too. Your free spirit and "color outside the lines" attitude inspire Mommy to live the same way. Never boxed in but living fully alive in Christ! I love you my son, you are a boy after God's heart.

Finally, this dedication is also to that exhausted, overwhelmed, shell of a person sitting alone on Grandma's old rocking chair in the wee hours of the night, tears streaming down her face wondering if her life would ever make a difference. Silently crying out to God as her newborn baby girl lay comfortably in her arms, questioning the promises He made to her over a decade prior. To that new mom who, with each crinkled smile and gentle coo, began feeling living water bubble up from within again, while falling madly in love with her newborn baby girl. To the *Me* who wondered if God would remember His promises after nearly half my life had passed since He made them—this book is for you! God's promises are yes and amen! If He made the promise, it's not a matter of *if* He'll fulfill it but *when*. This book is evidence that the *when* doesn't so much matter, it's that we never let go and never stop pursuing the promise that matters most. *God thinks you can do anything…*

ACKNOWLEDGMENTS

To my amazing family who has loved me, prayed for me and supported me throughout my life, and specifically, as I've ventured into this new season. To my mom and Rick, who selflessly give of their time to hang out with their grandkids so I could meet deadlines and pursue my dreams. Mom, your life beautifully demonstrates what love looks like and I thank God for a mother who has shown me how to live selflessly and give unconditionally. To my grandparents, Jim and Nancy, who pray for me, and my family, daily—you lead by example what it is to bear fruit with your life and give generously to others. Thank you all so much for your sacrifice and for your love, I couldn't have done any of this without you.

To my dad and Susan, I love you both so much and thank God for you! Dad, you raised me to go for the impossible. One of the earliest memories I have is at four years old sitting on your lap in the big brown chair accepting Jesus in my heart as my Lord and Savior. I'll never forget the warmth radiating from you as you imparted in me the love of my Heavenly Father through Christ Jesus. You are my hero, Dad. Your perseverance through life, your trust in the Father, and your undeniable connection to the heart of God...I always have and always will admire you. I thank God for you, Dad.

To my amazing in-laws, the Johnston/Nelson/Martinez/Bode Bunch...I love you and am so thankful for such an amazing, Jesus-loving, God-fearing extended family! Each of you inspires me in different ways. To my mother-in-law Carole, you are a light in the darkness shining bright the love of Jesus. Your fearlessness to walk into the darkest of places, boldness in standing for truth and gentleness in loving even the most unlovable *(which has been me at times!)* have influenced my life and challenged me to do the same...*it's all about Jesus.*

In loving memory of my grandma Virginia (Jackie) Torkildson, my great-grandmother Katherine Cranford and my father-in-law Leon Nelson, each of you inspired me in some special, unique way. I love you and am thankful you are rejoicing in Heaven!

To Jeri, thank you for taking me under your wing and loving me, walking with me, teaching me, and believing in me. I thank God for such a beautiful mentor and friend. You are a bright light for Jesus and a beacon of hope to all who are lost and hurting. You are the "real deal" and I admire you greatly. I love you!

To Mary and Christina, your friendship breathed new life into me! I am thankful for your solid, godly, encouraging, life-giving friendship! You are my sisters and you love me just as I am. Your lives inspire me to run, not walk, into the Father's arms where I find rest. You beautifully model the nature of Christ through your humility, your gentleness, and your fierceness! I am a better person for knowing you both.

To Dr. Sandy, thank you for dedicating your life to the message of the cross! God intersected our paths at just the right time and I could not be more appreciative to you for all you've invested in me—time, prayer, love and friendship, most importantly, you were instrumental in bringing the cross back as the central focus of my heart and ministry. I love you and thank God for you!

To the amazing team at Destiny Image for believing in me, and the message of this book—Larry Sparks and Sierra White, you could see something underneath the obvious and stepped out into the unknown with me to create this book. As I began my publishing journey several years ago, I prayed that God would guide me to just the right company who would know how to help steward the message in my heart. I'll never forget reading through the About" page on your website as I felt the presence of God come over me and I wept. In that moment I knew that *you* were the publishing house for me. Sierra—you have been an absolute joy to work with! I couldn't have asked for a better, more compassionate, considerate person to guide me through the publishing process. John Martin, thank you for your creative insights and helping shape the final elements of the book! To the entire creative team at Destiny Image, from the title of the book to the beautiful cover design to every process and detail in between, I have nothing but the highest of praise for you! Larry, you encouraged me to simply write the book God had already penned in my heart and throughout my life. I thank God for you all!

Finally, thank you, Jesus. My Lord and Savior. My Best Friend. You have walked with me all the days of my life and have carried me through every tough season. Nothing is impossible with You! To God be all the glory and honor and praise for the compilation of this book. It's His-story and He's invited me in.

CONTENTS

FOREWORD

Krissy called me one day and asked if she could come by my office, not far from where she lives in Pensacola, FL. As we spent time together talking about everything, it was evident that she "walked in the Spirit." It was oozing from her, the very presence of God.

She desires Him above all else. When she is alone He is there; when she is with her family, He is there; when she is walking through life, she is aware of Him and what He wants to do through her; when she is in church, she is caught up in His presence. She wants to listen to Him and be willing to obey His every request.

When each one of my kids were born, I asked them, "What was it like when God was making you?" Of course, they couldn't answer me but it doesn't change the fact of what the Bible says:

> *For you created my inmost being; you knit me together in my mother's womb.* —Psalm 139:13

I believe that from the very moment that a person is born, God is on a mission to draw us into a relationship with Him. Unfortunately, there are millions of other voices out there to keep us from knowing Him. We are raised in homes that don't mention Christ at all. People become bitter from abuse, and blame God. They decide to go down a path doing what is right in their own eyes. They are influenced by people around them. They look for advice from those around them. As God speaks to them, they shut the door, not wanting to listen. They start feeling worthless, looking for someone to accept them.

We have to be a light in this world to those who are living in darkness. We have to be ready to give an answer to the hope that is in us. We have to bring Christ to the forefront of people's minds. That He is the one who brings healing to the hurts. We have to be the ones that bring a good influence of a powerful God. We have to let them know that Jesus Christ accepts them and has a plan for their lives.

As we stir up the things of God in people's lives, they will desire more of Him. He then can peel away the layers of hurt, blame, and bitterness, and open up a whole new life for them in Christ.

Krissy has such a gift with words, they come alive on the page. It is so evident that she lives in a relationship with the King of kings and Lord of lords. It stirs a desire for God in people's lives so that they too can experience HIM and let Him flow through them to others.

Father, I pray that you move by your Spirit and take this book to give hope to people. You want to KNOW them and you want them to KNOW you. Do a mighty work transforming lives and letting them know there is SO much more to living for you…it is a relationship. AMEN!

JERI HILL
Widow of Steve Hill
President & Minister of
Together in the Harvest Ministries/Steve Hill Ministries
Gulf Shores, AL

Introduction

COME FOLLOW ME

Do you ever find yourself longing for those "simpler" days? For that guiding hand of a parent to quietly slip into yours and guide you toward your destiny? For the comfort of a friend to come alongside you in life's most hectic of moments and whisper those priceless words of affirmation, *"You're not alone"*? Well, thankfully there *is* a hand you can hold! A hand of One who walks beside you through your journey and One who will pick you up and carry you when times are really tough. A hand of One who will **never** let go. It's *Jesus*.

> *Be strong and courageous. Do not be afraid or terrified because of them, for the LORD your God goes with you; he will never leave you nor forsake you.* —Deuteronomy 31:6

From the moment you were conceived in the womb to the day you take your very last breath on earth—God is with you! God is with you through all the ups and downs, through the hurt and pain of your past and through each and every one of your successes and failures. He loves you so, *so* much.

Recently, I had an encounter with the Lord that caused my perspective to dramatically shift because I was given the incredible opportunity to see *through* the eyes of Jesus. This was an encounter where Jesus came into the room and took me by the hand. He came to me and He brought me *back* to some familiar moments in **His** story. This is the day Jesus took me by the hand. The day He allowed me to feel what He felt and see what He saw. Please, open your heart now as you come along with me on this journey.

THE DAY JESUS TOOK ME BY THE HAND

This is the day Jesus came into the room and took me by the hand. He said to me gently, "*Come follow me*." Naturally, I assumed He meant to come follow Him onward into my destiny, into the plans He has for my life…but His meaning far exceeded what I could comprehend. He wanted me to follow Him *back*—back into moments in history when He walked the earth.

First, we were at the well with the Samaritan woman. I saw the well. I could see down into its depths. This is where He had me focus. Down deep into the dark depths of the well where no bottom was in sight. I knew what was happening around me…Jesus was there…and He was talking to the woman. I could hear Him. I could feel His compassion and love. I was there with them. I could feel the woman's fear as she worried about the life she had lived. Dark and empty like the well I was in. I could feel into her heart and the emptiness she felt. And then as they talked…I could *feel* the waters of hope rushing in as Jesus said to her, "*I am the living water*." Her regret and her pain tried to rise up like a pail in the well, drawing from the depths of her despair all of the reasons His living water shouldn't be allowed to enter her heart. But the force of His love for her was too strong, *she couldn't fight it*—not with her stories of all the husbands she had had, not even with the weight of the guilt she had carried on her for so long. Nothing could stop the power of the waters of His reviving and refreshing love that poured out for her in that moment. I was able to feel the deep focus Jesus had for her. She was the one.

She was the only *one* who mattered in that moment. Her testimony would shake history.

Next, He brought me to the woman who touched the hem of His garment. I was there with Him as He pressed through the crowd. I could feel His deep focus as He moved through the crowd of people, knowing where and to *whom* He was headed. Then, suddenly, I could feel the moment His focus shifted as power left from His body. **Someone had touched Him!** Someone had drawn power from His body. Someone with faith the size of a mustard seed, who knew the authority He carried. I could see through His eyes and feel through His heart as He quickly and intensely shifted His gaze from where He was going to finding **the one** who had touched Him. Then as He looked down low—there on the ground—there she was. This woman, this *precious woman* who had a need. She needed a complete physical healing. And she had gotten it! I could feel the moment Jesus determined to affirm her and the faith she had. Faith that had drawn power from His body like drawing water from a well. I was there as He knelt down low to speak those words to her that would shake all of history, *"Daughter, your faith has made you well."*

Then, knees trembling, I saw the woman on the ground as she was about to be stoned. I could feel the urgency in the heart of Jesus as He ran to her to protect her. She was, after all, His precious child—one of His sheep. Somehow she had gotten out of the pasture but here He was, Jesus, the Shepherd—*her* shepherd—and He had found her. She had almost gotten away from Him. But He had reached her just in time to rescue her and bring her home. I could feel the moment as the dirt stirred in the air as He lunged to her. It was heavy. There He covered her and said those incredible words that would shake history, *"If any of you is without sin let Him cast the first stone."* No one could. And she was safe. I could feel the moment as relief settled over Jesus—His beloved daughter was safe in His arms.

Finally, I was in the most excruciating place I could ever fathom. As I looked out I could tell I was looking through the eyes of Jesus, the Lamb being slain. I was staring out through His eyes on the cross peering over the land. Gazing longingly down at His people—the ones crucifying Him. I was there and could feel the tears welling up in His eyes as His heart cried out with compassion, *"Father, forgive them! They don't know what they are doing."* I could feel the deep emotion of the Lamb being slain. The pain. The agony. The remorse for His precious children who had no clue what they were doing. They were blinded by sin. They couldn't see. But then welling up inside was the deepest of emotion, like a bubbling of living water. It was like the water I could feel rushing *into* the woman at the well. ***It was joy.*** Joy was overwhelming the heart of the Lamb as He reflected on the promise of God that this act was going to tear that veil and His people were finally going to be able to see. To see Him, the Lamb, the Messiah, slain for the entire world. For all sin, for all time, once and finally,d the Lamb of God proclaims, ***"It is finished"***! And then a deep relief as the pain lifted and His spirit and my spirit were taken away from this defining moment in history. Now and forevermore the children of God have a way to the Father's heart. A way was made for us to run into the Father's arms. And I was free. The curse was broken. And now the entire world could know that Jesus is Lord. Jesus is Savior. Jesus is the Lamb of God slain from the very foundations of the earth—just for *you*. You are the *one* in ***His***-story.

That is the day Jesus took my hand and walked me through *His*-story. The day He took my hand and allowed me to feel what He felt and see what He saw. It was His-story…but He let me in.

DARE TO BELIEVE

Are you longing for an encounter with Jesus? Do you long to see how you fit into His-story? Do you realize that encounters with God are available to you in your everyday life? God longs to be near you and have you lean your head against His chest. He desires fellowship with you friend! Jesus died so that all might come near to the Father (see Eph. 2:13)!

*God declares over you right now, "You will seek me and **find Me** when you seek me with all your heart"* (Jer. 29:13).

I encourage you to take a moment and examine your heart. Do you feel a deep hunger for more of God welling up in you right now? Maybe you've been feeling it for some time. Perhaps this is something new for you. Please know that God wants to meet with you today. I believe the stirring you've been feeling within is confirmation that you are in the right place and you have picked up the right book in the right season of your life. So, press on and join me in this journey. God has a plan for you. He desires to show you how and where you fit in *His*-story.

He longs to take you by the hand and show you He has always been there for you, that He has good things for you, and that He thinks you can do anything! As His child, you have His life-giving Spirit inside of you! He desires to give you a new perspective today, friend! Fresh lenses to see the good plans He has for you. *Are you ready?*

CREATED FOR THE IMPOSSIBLE

This book is for those who would dare to dream with God. Regardless of age, denomination, and education—God can and will use you to impact the world around you in your everyday life. For those of you who would be so bold as to simply *believe* the promises of God in your life and accept that He has good things for you. God uses every day, imperfect people to reflect the perfection of Christ to a world desperate for hope! Desperate for answers! Desperate for a Savior! Friend, if God can use me, He can use you too! If the dreams He has placed in my heart can come true, then so can the dreams in your heart. This is the reality of His plan. God wants to use you. He says over you today,

"For I know the plans I have for you," declares the Lord,
"plans to prosper you and not to harm you, plans to give

you hope and a future. Then you will call on me and come and pray to me, and I will listen to you. You will seek me and find me when you seek me with all of your heart."
—Jeremiah 29:11-13

Jesus takes us by the hand. He leads us beside still waters and He quiets our soul. He calls us out of the boat atop the waters of the impossible—our destiny—where we lock eyes with Jesus, trusting Him every step of the way. His focus is on *you*, friend! God thinks you can do anything! You were created for the impossible! God went through great lengths to make the impossible, possible in your everyday life! He sent His Son as the spotless, perfect Lamb of God to pay the penalty for sin once and for all so that you could be restored as His beloved child, coheir *with* Christ to everything the Father has. Please, as you read will you allow the Holy Spirit to stir up your faith and broaden your perspective of how God sees you?

What is He saying to you?

At the end of each chapter you'll notice a place where you can jot down what you're hearing the Holy Spirit speaking to you. Use this time to pause and simply listen. What is *God* saying to you? What is stirring in your heart? Write it down! Identify those thoughts of fear, unbelief, and shame that have burdened you for so long and exchange them for what *God* is speaking over you. Watch as He begins to shift your beliefs about Him and about yourself into proper alignment with the His Word of truth for your life!

> *But when he, the Spirit of truth, comes, he will guide you into all the truth. He will not speak on his own; he will speak only what he hears, and he will tell you what is yet to come.* —John 16:13

As we transition to Chapter 1, I want to leave you with a word from the Lord. This word God spoke to me when I was 15 years old.

This was *His* narrative over my life: He chose me, and He was asking me to do the same. *"Who will you choose?"* was His question. Here I was, a 15-year-old girl teetering between two worlds and I had a choice to make. That day I exchanged the narrative the enemy was using to confuse my identity and rob my purpose, with what God was saying about me! This word broke so much shame, confusion and doubt off of me. And it continues even to this day. Because the reality is, each and every day we have a choice to make, friend. He longs that we choose Him. That we lay down our lives before Him as willing vessels and simply say, "I choose you today God because *I love you.*"

FIRST WORD FROM THE LORD: MAY, 1998

I love you, My children. I made you, I created you, you are Mine. Do all that you can for me—TIME IS SHORT! The devil wants you to come home with him, I want you to come home with Me…who will you choose? I will give you peace, love, and happiness (joy) with eternal treasures in Heaven. The devil will give you only misery, hatred, and grief with eternal pain in hell…who will you choose? I made you, I created you, I need you…who will you choose? Choose life not death; I love you, choose Me.

PART 1

Laying The Foundation

Chapter 1

GOD CARES FOR YOU

*I praise you because I am fearfully
and wonderfully made; your works are
wonderful, I know that full well.*
—PSALM 139:14

Have you ever sat down and pondered the depths of God's care for you? Have you thought about the lengths He went through to create you? Have you considered the thoughts of God as He intricately knit you together in your mother's womb? Was He imagining all the things you would do in your lifetime—your first steps, first words, your first heartache, your first job, that moment when you accepted Jesus as your Lord and Savior? What about the moment when you realized He is a good Father and has good things for your life?

> *You made all the delicate, inner parts of my body and knit me together in my mother's womb. Thank you for making me so wonderfully complex! Your workmanship is marvelous—how well I know it. You watched me as I was being formed in utter seclusion, as I was woven together in the dark of the womb. You saw me before I was born. Every day of my life was recorded in your book. Every moment*

was laid out before a single day had passed. —Psalm 139:13-16 NLT

I believe that as a mother-to-be joyfully knits together tiny baby booties imagining the feel of each little toe that will soon slip into that delicate slipper, so God dreams over us as He forms us in our mother's womb! The Word of God says that you are God's special treasure (see Deut. 7:6)! God cares for you, friend, and He cares about every last detail of your life. You were fearfully and wonderfully made! Everything God creates is with purpose.

> *How precious are your thoughts about me, O God. They cannot be numbered! I can't even count them; they outnumber the grains of sand! And when I wake up, you are still with me!* —Psalm 139:17-18 NLT

GOD CARES ABOUT THE SPARROW—HOW MUCH MORE DOES HE CARE FOR YOU?

> *Are not two sparrows sold for a penny? Yet not one of them will fall to the ground outside your Father's care. And even the very hairs of your head are all numbered. So don't be afraid; you are worth more than many sparrows.* —Matthew 10:29-30

Danger lies ahead of the disciples as they prepare to go out and preach the Kingdom. In this scripture, Jesus was coaching them before He sent them out. He equipped them for the dangers ahead and the persecution they would no doubt face by sharing about the sparrow to emphasize just how much God, their Father, cares for them. He tells them they don't need to be afraid—that even though He (Jesus) isn't physically going with them on the journey, they won't be alone—God will be with them. It's interesting that Jesus uses God's care for the sparrow to communicate His deep love and care for His disciples. Sparrows in those days were considered to be useless! They were the most insignificant bird on the market. They were so common merchants would sell two sparrows for one penny, and five sparrows for two pennies—essentially offering the fifth sparrow for free.

> *Are not five sparrows sold for two pennies? Yet not one of them is forgotten by God....Don't be afraid; you are worth more than many sparrows.* —Luke 12:6-7

The *penny* in this scripture was a Roman *asarion,* which was worth a measly 1/16 of a silver denarius. Jesus is conveying a powerful message here, friend! That what man deemed so insignificant as to *throw in* an extra few sparrows for free, "*Here, take a few more,*" God deems valuable enough to notice if even one of them were to fall to the wayside. God has His eye on the sparrow...and He has His eye on you! *You matter to God.*

Do you ever wonder how God could notice *you* among the vast sea of people on the planet? Yet this scripture conveys His heart powerfully. Jesus is letting us know that God doesn't measure value the way man does. Man's value system determined that more sparrows equaled less value per bird. Yet if the sparrow were so common and insignificant why and how would God notice if even one fell to the ground? God values each of His creation uniquely. God declares, "Not only do I see each and every one of those sparrows, I care if even *one* falls to the ground. How much more I treasure you, the crown of My creation, that I would care to know the number of hairs on your head!" God's care for us and His value go deeper than we can ever fathom. He cares to know even the most seemingly insignificant detail about our lives!

> *And the very hairs of your head are all numbered.* —Luke 12:7 NLT

This facet of the heart of God speaks to me on a very personal and literal level because after I had my second child—only a year and a half after I gave birth to my first child—I lost *a lot* of hair! I'm talking *a lot!* This was a particularly vulnerable time in my life because I was still adjusting to my new identity as a mother. I didn't really know who I was anymore or what I was doing with my life. I had just transitioned from being a full-time career-minded businesswoman determined to climb the corporate ladder, to being a stay-at-home mom. My family and I had also made a cross-country move and were living with family for a season while we adjusted.

Between the pressures I felt from our big move, the hormones I was experiencing from being a new mom, and the sleep deprivation that came with having a newborn *and* a toddler, I was stressed out and exhausted most of the time! Meanwhile, handful after precious handful of my once long, full head of hair was falling out with every stroke of the brush. I was devastated! Our drains were constantly getting clogged while my amazing husband would faithfully and quietly declog the drain in our shower over and over again.

As trivial as it may sound, I found great comfort in knowing that I serve a God who would validate and affirm me in one of the most seemingly insignificant moments of my life. God cared so much about me that He was keeping count of how many hairs were actually *left* on my head! This was such a validating truth for me in those days, and still is today. It spoke the volumes Jesus intended it to in a very literal way. I could hear God's loving voice saying to me, *"Krissy. You may not feel like yourself right now but know that I am with you. I care about you. And therefore I care about what you care about. Cast all your burdens to Me, big or small. You matter to Me."*

God sees you right where you are, friend. He cares about you and He cares about what impacts your heart. It's in those moments when you feel insignificant to the world around you that you begin to appreciate just how treasured and adored you are by God. So be encouraged and allow the peace of God to rest on you; He will lift your head and replenish you with value and purpose today. Listen as He speaks words of truth and hope and peace and life over you now.

What is He saying? Take a moment and write it down. Cling to His Word for you, friend. Reflect on it often.

GOD IS NEAR TO THE BROKENHEARTED

The bigness and vastness of God always amazes me. Yet as we gleaned from the above passages, He cares about even the smallest of details in our lives. He is Creator of the inconceivably vast u erse and yet He knows us by name, knows the number of hair on our head, and wants to have a close, intimate relationship with us. It's extraordinary really. Ironically, it's in His careful attention to the smallest of details in our lives that points to His enormity. He is without borders. He is truly *in* everything! And in Him all things are held together (see Col. 1:17). What a mighty God we serve! David expresses his revelation on this very subject in the Psalms,

> *When I consider Your heavens, the work of Your fingers, the moon and the stars, which You have ordained, what is man that You are mindful of him, and the son of man that You visit him? For You have made him a little lower than the angels, and You have crowned him with glory and honor. You have made him to have dominion over the works of Your hands; You have put all things under his feet, all sheep and oxen—even the beasts of the field, the birds of the air, and the fish of the sea that pass through the paths of the seas. O Lord, our Lord, how excellent is your name in all the earth!* —Psalm 8:3-9 NKJV

God doesn't utilize our earthly scale to measure the *big* and *small* issues we face in life. God is concerned with what concerns us based on the impact on the hearts of His children. When your heart is breaking, God cares! When your spirit is crushed—He rescues you!

> *The Lord is near to the brokenhearted and saves the crushed in spirit.* —Psalm 34:18 ESV

The word *near* used in this passage is the Hebrew word *karov*, which means *"Close enough to touch."* God is close enough to touch when you are feeling brokenhearted! He is drawn to you! He comes near to you. Have you ever felt so discouraged you didn't know if you would ever feel joy again? Have you gone through something so devastating that you were left feeling totally crushed in spirit? I know I have. I can personally testify to the nearness of God in those times.

So how do you get out? How can this verse help you in your daily life? Let's go back into the story of the woman with the issue of blood. We briefly discussed her story in the introduction, which if you haven't yet read the introduction, this would be a good time to go back and read it for it sets the stage for the message of the entire book.

This woman had a debilitating physical illness that no doubt caused tremendous pain in her body, but also in the culture she lived in, would have caused her to be a total outcast from society. Can you imagine having an embarrassing and incurable physical illness and all the while, one by one, the people around you turned their back on you? This woman was desperate! She wanted freedom. Freedom from the physical illness, yes, but I imagine she would also have been desperate for freedom from the emotional pain and isolation this illness caused her as well. Let's take a look at her story,

> *Now when Jesus returned, a crowd welcomed him, for they were all expecting him. Then a man named Jairus, a synagogue leader, came and fell at Jesus' feet, pleading with him to come to his house because his only daughter, a girl of about twelve, was dying.*
>
> *As Jesus was on his way, the crowds almost crushed him. And a woman was there who had been subject to bleeding for twelve years, but no one could heal her. She came up behind him and touched the edge of his cloak, and **immediately** her bleeding stopped.*
>
> ***"Who touched me?"*** *Jesus asked.*

When they all denied it, Peter said, "Master, the people are crowding and pressing against you."

*But Jesus said, "Some**one** touched me; I know that power has gone out from me."*

*Then the woman, seeing that she could not go unnoticed, came trembling and fell at his feet. In the presence of all the people, she told why she had touched him and how she had been instantly healed. Then he said to her, "**Daughter**, your faith has healed you. Go in peace."* —Luke 8:40-48

Here we see Jesus immediately shift His focus when the woman touched His robe. He was intensely focused on where He was headed—to heal a dying 12-year-old girl—yet stopped the *instant* He felt power leave His body.

"Who touched me?"

With laser-ike focus He stopped to ask His disciples who touched Him! Someone had drawn near, *karov*—close enough to touch—with enough faith to pull from the life-giving power radiating from His body. Clearly this was unusual, as there were hundreds of people nearly crushing Him as He pressed through the large crowd. *This woman was different.* She was desperate and at the end of her rope. Brokenhearted and crushed in spirit after spending all the money she had on doctors, only to get worse.

She risked everything by coming out in public that day, but her faith was stirred within her spirit and she had *hope*. Against all odds this precious woman drew near to Jesus and in return Jesus drew near to her. She was crushed in spirit and He saved her. In doing so Jesus affirmed her faith and confirmed her healing!

What a wonderful reflection this is of the nature and character of God! God cares for you! He always has time for you. It doesn't matter what else is going on in the world—when you draw on Him in faith, He responds. *Seek and you will find.* Jesus transformed the story of her illness and rejection into a testimony of His limitless power and unconditional acceptance!

Do you have a need today? Are you desperate and at the end of your rope? Do you need Jesus to heal your body, your mind, or your heart? Reach out in faith today, friend. God cares for you. He desires to meet you right where you are.

Reach out your hand to Jesus...

Who touched me?

You may be dealing with a physical illness or maybe you've been battling with the sting of rejection for much of your life, or perhaps both. Wherever you are right now, take a moment and allow your heart to draw near to God. Let Him wash over you with His perfect peace and acceptance in order that you find the rest and healing and renewal that you so desperately need.

MY HEALING STORY

It was the spring of 1998—I was with my family visiting the Brownsville Revival in Pensacola, FL. God had been moving mightily in this church for about three years, and I was desperate! I was 15 years old and I was desperate for hope, desperate for peace, and desperate for someone to hold me and never let go. I could see God moving among the people in this thriving revival and I, like the woman with the issue of blood, longed to simply touch the hem of His robe. Not really knowing what to expect, I thought if I could get even just a sip of this life-giving water, I could survive another day. What I didn't realize at the time was that God had more than a sip in store for me...

As a young person I too felt desperate and at the end of my rope. I was an insecure teenage girl and I was tired of the constant pain I felt in my heart and the confusion and chaos swirling around in my mind. I was fed up with the relentless sense of rejection I felt from family and friends. I was tired of feeling like an outcast to my peers.

I was exhausted from the weight and burdens of life—family, school, church, loneliness. I felt like no one understood me. Like no one *really* cared enough to even try and understand me. I was beginning to wonder if God even cared. Because if He did, I couldn't fathom why I would feel so burdened and heavy **all** the time. What had begun in my preteen years as a small dose of typical teenage insecurity had blossomed into a full-blown identity crisis sprinkled with an overall sense of rejection and chronic case of isolation. I felt stuck somewhere in the middle of an unyielding game of tug-of-war over my soul.

I longed to encounter God. If He was real, then I needed to touch Him and I needed Him to speak into my life. But I had no idea what to even do.

While at the service, I saw people all around me passionately praying and worshiping. They were going after God. They were pursuing prayer and worshiping Him with joy; but as I stated before, I was *exhausted*. I stood off to the side, closed my eyes, and talked to God. I told Him I was tired. I said, "God, if you want someone to pray for me then please just send them to me...I'm not going to chase anyone around for prayer." Yes, I know the woman in our story above pushed through the crowd filled with faith to pursue Jesus and here I was basically saying I wouldn't push through the crowd of people around me to pursue prayer. But the thing is, my heart was pushing. Though my flesh was tired and my soul was weary, my spirit pushed through the walls around my heart as I talked to God. I could have stood there with a closed heart, but I didn't. I communicated with Him. And in doing so, my quiet, personal communion with God became the hand that reached out to touch the hem of His garment. I had *hope* that He was going to break through and save me. *And that is precisely what He did.*

As I stood there, a few people came around and prayed over me. Each time they did, I could feel my heart softening more and more until my slouched arms shifted upward in an extension of surrender. As I worshiped God, tears streamed down my face. My heart was beginning to melt. Then a man came over and prayed for me. He spoke a word from the Lord that shook me to the core. In an instant, four life-changing words surged from his heart and out of his mouth—"Mover! Shaker! History maker!" His Words pierced my heart like a boulder breaking through a dam! Suddenly I felt two strong yet gentle hands reach downward from the heavens and push me to the ground! The floodgate of my heart was open and I wept. All of my fears, pain, and anxiety flowed freely from my eyes like waters flowing through the banks of a raging river. I was sobbing, yes, but the peace I felt was beyond comprehension. What happened next forever changed my life and shaped my destiny.

God had drawn near to me and He was now holding me tightly in His arms of everlasting love. In a gentle whisper He began to speak. His Words breathed life into the very depths of my tired and weary soul. My heart felt alive! He declared His destiny and purpose for my life. Suddenly the tug-of-war for my soul was over and God had won. He won my heart that night—my *whole* heart. He pursued me with His immeasurable love and I would forever be His. Just as the woman who touched the hem of Jesus' garment was affirmed in her faith, so He affirmed me in mine. I always knew my life mattered to God. I always knew He had a plan for me. It was on this night, as He held me in His arms, that I finally *believed* it. He gave vision to the dreams in my heart and for the first time I could see! I could see what it looked like. I could feel it—my destiny. It became tangible. Something I could clench my fists around as I would run full speed ahead the race He marked out for me with perseverance—never alone, always hand in hand with Jesus, *my Best Friend.*

The next morning when I woke up I felt totally revived! I was a brand-new creation. The old had passed and the new had come. From that day forward I began dreaming with God. I was convinced that He cared for me. I knew He was a big God with a big plan for my life. I was forever moved and changed by the reality of His deep love and affection for me. I never looked back. My God was before me now and I knew that nothing could hinder His plan. I was overwhelmed with the reality that God is GOOD, God is REAL, and God is BIG!

You see, God took a young, broken, insecure girl and transformed her in an instant. He took all the pieces of my broken heart and put them back together again—stronger than ever! He came near to me. He breathed life into my dry, dead bones. He restored my purpose and branded me with the fire of His enormous love for me.

We serve a great big God, friend! A God who in all His infinite glory deeply desires one thing—*relationship with His beloved*. You are His beloved. Is He yours?

The desire of His heart is that you will draw near to Him and walk with Him, hand in hand, every day of your life. That you will love Him and put your trust in Him alone as you choose to accept that He cares deeply for you and is interested in every facet of your heart. This is one of several life-changing encounters I have had with my Heavenly Father. As you read on in this book, you will hear about more of my story. From that day on my story and His story became one and now the story of my life is the story of His.

> *I have been crucified with Christ and I no longer live, but Christ lives in me. The life I now live in the body, I live by faith in the Son of God, who loved me and gave himself for me.* —Galatians 2:20

YOU HAVE A STORY TO TELL

Friend, you too have a story to tell. What has Jesus done for you? How has He cleansed you from your past? How has He healed your broken heart? Do you think the woman with the issue of blood had any idea about the impact her story would have on each generation after her? No! You don't realize the impact of your story until you begin telling it and even then, you may never know the butterfly effect of your testimony. Regardless, it's important that you share your story!

It is critical that you allow the reality of God's tremendous love and care for you to move deep into the caverns of your heart. That it penetrates any walls you may have built up. Today is the day, friend— *why wait?* I encourage you to seize this moment right now and ask God to come crashing into your heart with His perfect love that casts out all fear (see 1 John 4:18)!

Like a boulder to a dam, invite Him now to inhabit the depths of your heart with the fire of His unconditional love for you! I've heard it said before that love can move mountains, well, Love has a name, and it's Jesus and not only does He move mountains, He formed them! God can do anything, and right now He longs to woo your heart revealing to you His great care for you.

WE'RE ON A JOURNEY

The journey we are on in this book begins with a restoration of your faith in the depths of God's loving care for you. To have eyes that can see and ears that can hear the tender nature in which He desires you. God sees you, friend, right where you are in your life, and He calls you worthy. He gazes at you with eyes rich in compassion and says, "I don't see you the way everyone else sees. I don't look down on you with eyes of ridicule and judgment. I gaze at you with eyes of mercy and love. I examine your heart and I see *greatness* inside there. I see beauty. I see a home. Though you may feel insignificant at times, you are my special treasure. I call you valuable. I call you radiant. And with Me *nothing* is impossible!"

God cares for you...

What is He saying to you?

_____

_____

_____

_____

Chapter 2

GOD'S VOICE

*My sheep hear my voice, and I know
them, and they follow me.*
—JOHN 10:27 ESV

Though I encountered God for the first time at 15 years old, the first time I heard Him speak to me, *really* speak to me, was just after my 14th birthday. It was also the first time I had ever really cried out to Him. His voice forever altered the course of my life, dramatically shifting the way I saw myself, my interactions with others, and my relationship with Him personally. It surprises me, and quite frankly breaks my heart, how many believers are unaware that they too can hear directly from God through the Holy Spirit. We are His sheep and our ears are tuned to the sound of His voice by the Holy Spirit within us.

My sheep hear My voice...

When Jesus died on the cross and finished what He was sent into the world to accomplish, it meant the veil, *the barrier*, between those who believe in God and God Himself was ripped in two, from top to bottom (as only God could do), forever releasing His presence into the whole earth! There is now *nothing* that separates you, the believer, from your Heavenly Father! You can hear Him, know Him, and encounter Him in your everyday life!

> *But now in Christ Jesus you who were once far away have been brought near through the blood of Christ.* —Ephesians 2:13

To some, personally hearing God's voice might seem impossible, but thankfully it's what you were created for! You were created to hear and *know* the voice of God! I'm not saying that I fully understood the ins and outs of the access available to me at the age of 14, but what I did know was that something inside of me was longing for something real. I was desperate for someone bigger than the issues I was facing, someone who had the power to speak into my life and change my heart giving me new lenses to view the world from. Though I didn't articulate it in this way when I was a kid, deep down this is what I hungered for! So I cried out to God one day! From the depths of my soul I cried out and He answered me! God is real! He answered the cry of my heart, speaking into my identity and purpose, giving me direction for my life! I'll share the details of this a little later in the book.

FELLOWSHIP WITH THE FATHER

We were created for fellowship with the Father. In the very beginning sin severed our interaction with God, separating us from Him, but Jesus restored all and we can now approach Him freely and with confidence (see Eph. 3:12)! Where once priests and prophets seemed to be the only humans who could hear from God and communicate what He was saying, we now know that each of us can commune directly with the Father and hear directly from Him. *Why*, because we are His sons and daughters. We are His kids. And He is a good Father. Out of His immeasurable love for humanity, He sent His Son to save us and restore relationship!

This is how much God loved the world: He gave his Son, his one and only Son. And this is why: so that no one need be destroyed; by believing in him, anyone can have a whole and lasting life. God didn't go to all the trouble of sending his Son merely to point an accusing finger, telling the world how bad it was. He came to help, to put the world right again. Anyone who trusts in him is acquitted; anyone who refuses to trust him has long since been under the death sentence without knowing it. And why? Because of that person's failure to believe in the one-of-a-kind Son of God when introduced to him. —John 3:16-18 MSG

Growing up, I saw how everything my earthly father did was motivated by his love for me. Whether in making difficult choices, doing what he felt was best for me, making sure I was safe, or even in having fun together, his love for me was what motivated him. As I've gotten older, I have seen his consistency in this. Obviously, he's made mistakes through the years and he would be the first to admit as much, but mistakes or not, his driving force has always been the same—love. His deep desire to keep me safe, see me succeed, and do well influenced his every decision. I'm so thankful to have a good dad.

Our Heavenly Father is all knowing. He is omnipotent. He knows all and is in all. Unlike an earthly father, He doesn't make mistakes; but like a good earthly father, He is driven by His love for us, period. God is good. He is a good Father. And hearing His voice is just one of the beautiful facets of our relationship with Him.

I know firsthand one of my dad's greatest joys in life is fellowship with me. When our lives create a geographical distance between us, my dad longs to communicate with me. We text, we call, we Skype, and we even email! Communication with my dad is one of my favorite things in life as well. I know that my dad is proud of me. I know that he loves me. I know he wants what is best for me, and he challenges me...he makes me want to be a better person.

Friend, do you realize your Heavenly Father wants a close, personal relationship with you—a relationship where you communicate with one another. He longs for a deep, intimate fellowship with you for no other reason than because you are His child and He loves you with a fervent, intense love. He didn't create you so that you could check tasks off of His eternal "to-do" list. He's not a taskmaster. You were made out of love, for love, and to love. The Pharisees had a difficult time with this concept. They were so accustomed to things being *complicated* that when Jesus came in with such simple truth, they were constantly challenging Him. They were convinced Jesus was behaving contrary to the Law, and they were determined to catch Him stumbling.

In the Book of Matthew, we see the Pharisees question Jesus regarding the most "important" of the commandments. They want to know what, from their massive "to-do" list, is the chief element to following God. Essentially they are saying, *"Alright, if you really are sent from God, you're going to have a really good answer as to which of these commandments is the most significant. Surely your response will be deeply profound and analytical and it will make sense to us."*

> *"Teacher, which is the great commandment in the law?"*
> *Jesus said to him, "'You shall love the Lord your God with*
> *all your heart, with all your soul, and with all your mind.'*
> *This is the first and greatest commandment. And the second*
> *is like it: 'You shall love your neighbor as yourself.' On these*
> *two commandments hang all the Law and the Prophets."*
> —Matthew 22:36-40

I love what Jesus is saying here! Everything—the law and the prophets—hinges on LOVE. Loving God, loving people, and loving yourself.

Jesus wouldn't be trapped by the Pharisees' trick questions. *He couldn't!* Jesus was the word made flesh (see John 1:14). Part of Jesus' mission on the earth was to demonstrate for us the nature of God. He walked in love, peace, patience, compassion, mercy, and righteousness. What the Law couldn't accomplish, which was to show us exactly what a godly, upright life *looked* like, Jesus came into the world and modeled perfectly. He was fully God and yet fully man. Jesus relied on His fellowship and communion with the Father to reflect God's true nature in the world. He was often found praying and fasting, and He was filled with the Holy Spirit who helped Him live the life God desires His children to live. Jesus beautifully demonstrates what the life of the believer looks like. Slipping away to commune with the Father in secret, in the quiet, relying on His guidance by hearing and knowing His voice, bearing the fruit of the Spirit in His life. This was His story. So here's a question for you: if Jesus prioritized and relied on His fellowship with the Father while He was on the earth, how much more should we?

Nothing Can Separate You From God's Love

And I am convinced that nothing can ever separate us from God's love. Neither death nor life, neither angels nor demons, neither our fears for today nor our worries about tomorrow—not even the powers of hell can separate us from God's love. No power in the sky above or in the earth below—indeed, nothing in all creation will ever be able to separate us from the love of God that is revealed in Christ Jesus our Lord.
—Romans 8:38-39 NLT

It is important for us to realize that nothing, *NOTHING*, can separate us from the Love of God revealed to us through Christ Jesus. Not troubles or persecution or pain or heartache or even our mistakes—past or present. Not even your will! You may choose to have nothing to do with God and may even deny Him but even that will never change the fact that He will always love you! If God's love for us were contingent on our behavior, He would never have sent His

Son to die for us! God didn't send His Son for perfect people, He sent His perfect Son to redeem sinners and restore us to right standing with Himself so that He could be in fellowship with us. This was His plan from the very beginning of time. Through His death we also die to our flesh and through His resurrection and life we are made alive with Christ (see Eph. 2:5).

This is foundational in hearing the voice of God. Establishing this baseline—*His great love for us*—is key to you beginning to hear His voice more clearly and plainly and on a regular basis in your day-to-day life. In order to hear Him more clearly, it's important to realize how deeply He loves you and desires fellowship with you! From here you can begin to fall deeper in love with Him. Hearing Him becomes a beautiful result of your relationship with Him. Suddenly you'll find yourself doing "normal" day-to-day tasks all while conversing with God. Just as my husband and I visit with each other while cleaning, cooking, and eating, so you can have daily fellowship with God during these same tasks. It's so fun!

I have worked with and met many people who simply cannot fathom that God even loves them. Let alone wants to speak to them. Having volunteered the last several years at my local Teen Challenge Women's Center, I have had the privilege of getting to know so many of the amazing women in the program. They have similar stories in that most enter Teen Challenge broken down, chewed, and spit out by the world. Many are convinced that any chance they may have had for God to love them has surely ceased. It's a remarkable thing to watch as the days, weeks, and months go by and they begin to heal and learn of God's love for them. It's such a joy to witness as the love of God begins to wash over them. I'll be reading a scripture, sharing a story, singing a song (*which can be scary—I'm not going to lie*), or praying over them and I'll watch as God's amazing love and grace covers over the women as a warm blanket on a cold day. Tears begin streaming down their cheek as they accept that He loves them, He *really* loves them, and they surrender to that love, receiving it for the first time, or the first time in a long time. It is a gift to be a part of such a thing. I deeply desire to help people see themselves the way God sees them.

I'll never forget one day as I was spending time with the Lord preparing to speak at one of their chapel services. I was struggling to know what I was to share with them. It can be easy to over-prepare when most often speaking from the heart and from a place of testimony is the most effective. I try to avoid being overly theological because it's not head knowledge that is going to mend their broken hearts and broken lives, it's the presence of God. It's His living word and His life-giving breath! Therefore, I come before the Father with an open heart, He knows what they need, and I listen. On this particular day God spoke clearly to me and said, *"Krissy, your only job is to help them fall madly in love with me."*

Wow. What an honor. *Yes Lord!* What a joy to help the women fall madly in love with God by sharing about His goodness. His nature. His deep love for *them*! That there is nothing at all in the world that can separate them from His love! Not their past mistakes, not their present sin, not anything! They simply need to surrender their life, giving Him permission to invade their heart with His love.

> *The Lord is close to the brokenhearted and saves those who are crushed in spirit.* —Psalm 34:18

One day while driving in my car I began thinking about broken hearts. I thought about the goal of the Father and the goal of the enemy of our hearts. The Holy Spirit began to show me how the enemy's objective is to shatter our hearts, leaving them crushed, fragile, and timid while building up strong defensive walls around them; but God's objective is to shatter the *walls* while building up a strong, whole, and courageous heart within us!

Think about that for a moment, the enemy wants to crush our hearts and build up strong defensive walls surrounding and imprisoning our broken, fragile hearts within. We end up walking around as high-functioning broken people because we don't allow anything to penetrate the walls. Why would we? Our hearts are broken. Our instinct is to protect what is broken inside, not realizing that we are inadvertently keeping God out as well. Meanwhile, God's goal is to come crashing in with His perfect love, destroying that wall in order to restore our heart, making it whole again. Stronger than ever before!

As you give God even the slightest of openings, He will rescue, repair, and rebuild your wounded and weary heart. If you'll look close enough, you'll discover that the wall around your heart has a door and you have the authority to open it to God or keep it closed. Choose to open it, friend, and Abba God will come crashing in with His love destroying the wall once and for all while restoring your soul. God is here! He is the lover of your soul. Reach out your hand. Let hope in. I made a choice a long time ago that though I may feel pain deeply and often, I'd still much rather live with an open, exposed heart allowing people in than live with a closed heart surrounded by walls keeping people, *and God*, out. God can use an open, vulnerable heart. He will also protect it. His very name means *protector!* He is *Jehovah Nissi*—God my Banner—my covering, my protector, my victory! God covers our heart with His love and is quick to heal if we are wounded…we just need to let Him.

CLING TO THE WORD OF THE LORD

As I mentioned in Chapter 1, after my first real encounter with God at 15 I was never the same. I had opened the door to my heart and let God in. I encountered His amazing love firsthand. And I felt like a daughter…like a child of God. But somehow through my 20s, I drifted from the intimacy I knew so deeply in my youth. Life looked different than I imagined it would. I found myself frequently discouraged. I was in a career I never thought I would be in and began climbing the corporate ladder, causing my focus to shift from the visions God had shown me for my life to more of a corporate "career-path" way of thinking. I was still in love with Jesus but my ambitions were different. All the while, on the inside I was becoming more and more dry. The passion I once had for God shifted to passion for the industry I was working in. Still, deep down I was tired and a bit frustrated. I was trying so hard to "become" something that I was draining my strength. I was emptying myself into something *good* but deep down I sensed it wasn't God's best for my life.

Looking back, I realize my frustration was rooted in my resolve that *this was it.* I sort of gave up because I just assumed I would be doing this forever. I wasn't really seeking God any more. Because I couldn't understand what God was doing, I reinterpreted His promise to look more like what I was doing right then, rather than seeing this as merely part of the process to where He was taking me. There was still growth needed to take me to the next step in His plan, and I didn't realize this was all part of it. I stopped seeking Him and began settling. I traded in my God promise for my current circumstance!

Friend, cling to the word of the Lord in your life! Hold fast to the promises God has given you! Seek God daily! Never settle for your own interpretation of His promise, wait upon the Lord and listen to His voice.

Know that God will use everything in your current circumstance for your good and His glory, but never settle. If deep down you know that there is more, that God has shown you more—cling to that! Don't stop believing that what God has shown you will come to pass. If God promised it to you, it's not a matter of *if* but *when*. Seek Him. Seek His face. And allow joy to invade your circumstance. You'll find that instead of surviving your day and tolerating the people around you, you'll begin to thrive in your day and love the people around you. God has you in this place right now for a reason…it's a stepping-stone along the path He has drawn out for your life. This is your story. And He is the author.

If you read through several of the stories in the Bible, you'll find a common theme of many years between the promise and the fulfillment. Joseph waited 17 years between his promise and fulfillment, and much of that time was spent in prison! David was on the run from Saul who wanted to kill him and all the while had a mantle of kingship on his life.

I wish I had this perspective in this dry season of my life. Though I prayed a little it was mostly motivated by the negative, "God—help me to survive the day…help me to be patient with those who drive me crazy! Help me to tolerate the people around me!" I couldn't see at the time that these prayers were survival based—even fear based—and were far from the relational fellowship I could have had with the Father.

Jesus said in John 10:10, "I have come to give you *life* and life to the full!" Let us be like Paul who learned to be content in all circumstances (see Phil. 4:11)! Just because you're waiting on the fulfillment to the promise, doesn't mean you can't live in peace today! Don't be so focused on the future that you can't appreciate the beauty happening right now, in the journey. What has God given you? Cling to the promise while still appreciating the here and now.

> *God, thank you for the promise you have spoken into my life! Thank you for my current job and all that I am learning! Thank you for your provision! Thank you for this season in my life! I'm clinging to Your promise, hoping for the future but I'm living where I'm planted today. I won't give up hope in Your promises and the dreams of my heart but I'll remain content in all circumstances, coming before you with a spirit of gratitude! Speak into my life today!*

When God speaks, dead things come alive! God speaks hope. He longs to speak to you. He desires that you be so close to Him that you begin to anticipate His voice. I believe He's stirring up a hunger inside of you to hear His voice and know Him more.

HIS GENTLE WHISPER

There came a point in Elijah's story when he was tired and at the end of his rope. He wanted to die. He had gone out into the wilderness, laid down, and asked God to take his life,

Elijah was afraid and ran for his life. When he came to Beersheba in Judah, he left his servant there, while he himself went a day's journey into the wilderness. He came to a broom bush, sat down under it and prayed that he might die. "I have had enough, Lord," he said. "Take my life; I am no better than my ancestors." Then he lay down under the bush and fell asleep. —1 Kings 19:3-5

Elijah needed an encounter with God. He was desperate! God sent an angel to call him from the wilderness, sending him on a journey for 40 days and 40 nights to Horeb, the mountain of God. Upon arrival, he went into a cave to sleep. Then the word of the Lord came to him again,

And the word of the Lord came to him: "What are you doing here, Elijah?"

He replied, "I have been very zealous for the Lord God Almighty. The Israelites have rejected your covenant, torn down your altars, and put your prophets to death with the sword. I am the only one left, and now they are trying to kill me too."

The Lord said, "Go out and stand on the mountain in the presence of the Lord, for the Lord is about to pass by."

Then a great and powerful wind tore the mountains apart and shattered the rocks before the Lord, but the Lord was not in the wind. After the wind there was an earthquake, but the Lord was not in the earthquake. After the earthquake came a fire, but the Lord was not in the fire. ***And after the fire came a gentle whisper. When Elijah heard it, he pulled his cloak over his face and went out and stood at the mouth of the cave.*** *Then a voice said to him, "What are you doing here, Elijah?"* —1 Kings 19:9-13

Elijah needed a fresh encounter with the presence of God and that came through His gentle whisper. How often do we get so bogged down by the pressures of life that we find we need to hear from God afresh and anew? We need to encounter Him. Elijah was the only follower of God left and he was being pursued by his enemies who wanted to kill him. He was truly alone. But God loved Elijah and knew what he needed. He sent out His Word to guide Elijah to the place of encounter.

The Word of God led Elijah to an encounter with the presence of God.

God has a place of encounter for each one of us. Maybe today it's in your living room or your closet or even your kitchen. Wherever you are you can encounter the presence of God! Encounters with God are for the everyday believer in our everyday life! He longs to speak to you, friend! And He knows just what you need. Pause for a moment and pray, *"God, I need you! I'm tired! I need to feel your presence! Speak into my life today!"* Now breathe and wait upon the Lord.

GOD'S FAMILIAR VOICE

It wasn't until I became pregnant with my first child that things began shifting for me. Something about this new life growing inside me seemed to cause the seemingly empty well within me to seep out living water that remained somewhere in the depths. As the months passed and I grew closer and closer to my due date, I could feel living water bubbling up in my spirit again. I was hungry for more of God. As I prepared my home for this new life that would soon be in the world, I could sense my heart was preparing for something new as well. A new baby, yes, but somehow I sensed there was some sort of a package deal about to be birthed.

The birth of my daughter indeed came with many surprises! I had no clue how dramatically life would change! The balance I had come to know and love was now suddenly *gone*! There was a new normal

I was struggling to adapt to! As joyful as the arrival of my baby was, it was as equally challenging—rich with emotional highs and lows! I would spend many nights weeping and crying out to God for help! For strength…wisdom…something *normal* I could cling to! It wasn't until this point that I could see how far I had gotten from that intimate place of relationship with the Father I had once known. I found myself reaching out for stability to what I had built throughout the last several years only to discover that there was nothing solid there. What I thought was a firm foundation was in reality sinking sand. My home, career, reputation, success…none of these could help me find refuge in this new season of the unknown. This was foreign soil. I didn't know what to do or who to turn to. *I felt so alone.*

Soon the time to return to work arrived a mere four weeks after giving birth. As the day grew closer, I would wake up in the night in sheer panic! My poor husband would sit up and just hold me as I wept. I realized the desires of my heart had changed. I no longer cared to climb that corporate ladder. I was a mother. I wanted to *be* a mother all day and every day. That was my purpose in life. There was no greater call, in my opinion, than this! I didn't want to go back to work and be in charge of anyone or anything. I felt desperate for clarity and direction.

This is when I finally began to dive back into the presence of God. For the first time in years I felt the bond between my Abba Father and me renewing. I was seeking Him and drawing near to Him. I was giving glory to God because I was utilizing the access Jesus died for me to have! In turn, He drew near to me. For the first time in a long time I realized how much I needed *Him*! Not just to tolerate people or survive the day…but I needed Him for breath! I needed Him for peace! I needed Him for love…for hope…for purpose…for *everything*! I was hungry for His presence…I yearned for His heart.

I was eager to hear His voice. I was desperate to hear Him speak into my life again in a fresh way. What was His plan for my life at this point with a new baby? I hadn't heard from Him in a while but I realized I also hadn't spent much time listening either. I hadn't spent much time pursuing Him and waiting on Him to respond.

Then I heard His familiar voice. Much like the word of the Lord came to Elijah in First Kings, His voice came to me as a gentle whisper and He was there. It was in the wee hours of the night as I rocked my new baby girl with tears streaming down my face that I finally surrendered my plans to Him and confessed I had no clue what I was doing!

"God…!" I cried.

"Speak into my life. Restore my purpose. Renew my identity in *You*. What do *you* want me to do? I can feel there is more! More than what I am doing. If you'll show me again, God, I promise you I will do it! Whatever it is!"

As I peered down at this precious baby in my arms it hit me. What she was doing there in my arms…lying there…existing as my child…*that* is what I was created to *do*. That is who I am in my Heavenly Father's eyes—*I'm His child*. I am His precious baby girl and He longed to hold me in His arms as He had done all those years ago and speak into my destiny afresh and anew.

THE WELL WITHIN

In the days and weeks to follow, as I released the reins of my life over to Him again, I began hearing His voice yet again. It was so familiar. I knew it so well. *"My sheep know my voice."* Pictures of my life began playing through my spirit as a movie trailer. Familiar pictures that He had shown me in my youth. If you can imagine those old movies that played from reels of film. It was as though the film reel of my life began playing again. I could see the books I would write. I could see my children playing and running around with their daddy. I could see my life as a mom. A wife. A writer. A speaker. Though no blueprints were given I knew that God had the plan. He had already written my story. I needed only to allow myself to be His child, rest in His arms, and surrender.

Suddenly I could smile again. I felt joy. Life was surging through my veins!

Friend, I wonder if you can to relate to my story. Do you feel as though the film reel of your story has stopped playing? Are you wandering around, sometimes aimlessly, longing for vision? Praying for purpose?

There's a well of living water inside you! When you gave your life over to God, the well within you was filled with His living water. Maybe you've been feeling dry, weary, lost, alone, empty...whatever the case may be, know this—there is *still* living water inside you. Your well may not be overflowing at this point but it sure can! Begin to talk to God. Begin to cry out to Him for more! God is real! Surrender your plans to Him! The Bible tells us that He is the Alpha and Omega, the First and the Last (see Rev. 22:13). He is limitless and His love for you is without borders! As you draw near to Him, He draws near to you and the walls of that well will begin to seep out the living water that is stored up in there deep into your soul! As you cry out for more of His presence in your life, He will fill that well with new life and with new water until you are overflowing. It's from this place of overflow that you are able to live the abundant life Jesus died for you to have!

> *The thief does not come except to steal, and to kill, and to destroy. I have come that they may have life, and that they may have it more abundantly.* —John 10:10 NKJV

His breath gives us life! His Word gives us peace and direction. John 15:4 states that when we abide in Him, He abides in us. We will discuss this more later but for right now please allow your heart to wrap around this truth: if you are desperate to encounter God and hear His voice, simply surrender and begin to listen to what He has to say to you.

Friend, God wants to begin speaking to you more. He has a message of hope for your situation. He has a message of peace for your circumstance. God thinks you can do anything! And sometimes that looks like us moving past our own limitations and believing what God says about us. He calls you beloved. He calls you His child. His friend. He desires your heart—your *whole* heart.

Just as sheep know the voice of their shepherd and follow him wherever he leads so your Heavenly Father desires that you know His voice following Him as He leads you to a place of fresh encounter today. *It's time to surrender...*

What is He saying to you?

Chapter 3

CHOOSING TO SURRENDER

*For you know that it was not with perishable
things such as silver or gold that you were redeemed
from the empty way of life handed down to you
from your ancestors, but with the precious blood
of Christ, a lamb without blemish or defect.*
—1 Peter 1:18-19

As I lay on the ground, face gazing up toward the heavens filled with a fresh wave of the Holy Spirit, I began to see a man in white walking toward me. Suddenly, I was on a dirt road in the middle of nowhere laying with my arms spread wide. I began to see this man in white with the heart of a father—warm, rich with compassion and love—reach down and pick me up. Still limp from this fresh blast of the Holy Spirit, my body hung like a rag doll across the arms of the Father...*Abba.*

He began walking with me. His eyes were fixed on where He was taking me. My body cradled gently in His strong arms as He stepped purposefully, yet gracefully, forward. The world around me began to brighten. Everything seemed to blur together into one crisp, yet warm, white cloud. As the Father carried me lovingly in His arms, my spirit was filled with wonder.

Where was He taking me?

I could see Him holding me as though I was watching a movie. I was utterly limp—arms, legs, head—practically paralyzed, but full of peace and warmth and love.

Then I began to see it…to see where we were going.

I saw *Him.*

Jesus.

The Lamb of God.

He was sitting on the throne and the Father was taking me to Him. My spirit leapt inside me yet again. Then we were there. We were before the Lamb. My body still flailed loosely in the Father's arms. I watched as the Father leaned down to lay me at the feet of the Lamb, saying to Him,

"Here I have found you another one…a life fully surrendered…a life laid down at the feet of My Son. Here I give You, My Son, the reward of your suffering."

Unable to move, I felt a tear stream down from both sides of my face as I gazed up upon the Lamb. Lying at His feet, I watched as He leaned His face down to look at me. *He was the Lamb*! He sat robed in glory crowned with many crowns. He looked down upon me and He smiled. His eyes sparkled with love, with compassion, and with excitement at this life laying in total abandon at His feet.

Gazing up at His beauty, I began to wonder what was going to happen next.

Only stares.

Stares straight into each other's eyes, *no*, hearts—somehow *both*.

I could see how much He loved me and I sensed He could see the same in me.

I closed my eyes and somehow I could hear into His heart, "I have known you since before the very foundations of the earth were formed and I always knew yours would be a life surrendered."

I opened my eyes to see a smile forming upon the face of the Lamb. I smiled and gazed longingly into His loving eyes.

Then I was able to speak, *"What are you doing Lord?"* I asked.

He only stared.

Then another question crossed my heart, *"What do you want me to say to them?"*

As this question left my heart, I could see all the people of the world. The adults. The children—*oh', the children*—I asked again, *"What do you want me to say?"*

He answered, "You speak of the cross. You speak of my Love."

I replied with a sigh, "OK, Lord. I will speak of the cross, which reveals your love. Your *deep love* for all the world."

He smiled.

Then He looked intensely into my eyes and said, *"Now GO!* Speak of the cross. Speak of My love."

And in an instant I was swept back up into the arms of the Father and brought back to the road He had found me on. This road, I realized, was the road I was called to walk. It is the path marked out for me before the very foundations of the earth were formed. And it's on this road that I am to *"run with perseverance the race marked out for us"* (Heb. 12:1).

GIVING JESUS HIS REWARD

Did you know that your life laid down and surrendered before the Lord gives Jesus the reward of His suffering? Think about it for a moment...Jesus came into the world to bind up the brokenhearted and set the captives free (see Luke 4:18). You, who were once dead in your sin, are made alive in Christ (see Eph. 2:5)! You have an opportunity to willingly yield your life to the One who formed you. The One who made you. You can choose to be a life that is surrendered to the will of the One who calls you by name. The One who wrote your story and appointed this hour and this season as the one you would live in *His*-story.

The above is an encounter I had with the Lord a couple of years ago. Obviously, it is one that, again, has forever transformed and defined my life! As believers we have an awesome opportunity to *choose* to surrender our life to the Lord Jesus. We are not robots. We are not made to or coerced into a life of surrender. We have been given a gift from our Creator God to *choose*.

Some notes I wrote down after this remarkable encounter were as follows:

- Jesus paid it all…how many of us have surrendered it all?

- God gives us free will, and the best choice we can make is to surrender our will to the will of the Father.

- A surrendered life gives Jesus, the Lamb of God, the reward of His suffering.

- The Holy Spirit gives us the ability to cry *"Abba, Father!"* (Rom. 8:15).

- Where the Spirit of the Lord is there is freedom!

- Jesus paid it all…what will you give in return?

CHOOSING TO SURRENDER

As Jesus and his disciples were on their way, he came to a village where a woman named Martha opened her home to him. She had a sister called Mary, who sat at the Lord's feet listening to what he said. But Martha was distracted by all the preparations that had to be made. She came to him and asked, "Lord, don't you care that my sister has left me to do the work by myself? Tell her to help me!" "Martha, Martha," the Lord answered, "you are worried and upset about many things, but few things are needed— or indeed only one. Mary has chosen what is better, and it will not be taken away from her." —Luke 10:38-42

God's voice led me to the place of surrender. As I shared in Chapter 2, it was when I began to turn the reins over to Him that I began hearing Him speaking into my life again—afresh and anew. Suddenly vision for my life was restored. Purpose was illuminated. And the more He spoke, the more I could feel the flame of my deep love for Him rekindled. Before long there was a fire inside of me that burned hotter and brighter than ever before. The love of God began to consume me. His voice was again shaping my identity. And now, like Mary, my heart's desire is to sit at His feet, worship Him, love Him, and listen to what He has to say.

My surrender fanned into flame the fire inside me that continues to grow more and more to this day! Daily I surrender and daily the flame inside me grows into an all-consuming fire! The more I let go and allow Him to steer my life, the more He illuminates the path before me one faithful step at a time.

This doesn't happen overnight, though. Living a surrendered life becomes a choice I have the privilege of making each and every day. Our ability to choose is just that, *a choice*. It isn't a burden. It isn't an obligation. God designed us with a free will. We have been given this amazing gift of choice. We choose how much of our life we give to Him. We choose how much of our time, our resources, and our love we give to Him. One of the greatest things we can do with our will is to choose to surrender it to God! To the very One who gave it to us in the first place!

I love the story of Mary and Martha. Jesus didn't enter their home and demand they sit at His feet and listen to Him speak. They were free to choose. For Martha, she was doing the customary thing in preparing the meal, but Mary chose something new. Her choice to sit at His feet was unheard of and a bit radical. I love that Jesus affirmed her choice by stating,

> *"Martha, Martha," the Lord answered, "you are worried and upset about many things, but few things are needed— or indeed only one. Mary has chosen what is better, and it will not be taken away from her." —*Luke 10:42

As Jesus affirms her bold but humble choice, He is causing a shift in perspective. Suddenly, all they knew about custom and the role they should play in their interactions with people, especially men in leadership—particularly a rabbi—is shifted! This only makes sense if Jesus is in fact the Son of God, which Mary must have had some sort of revelation of. Women didn't just sit at the feet of a rabbi and listen to him speak in those days. But Jesus takes this opportunity to affirm that while many things may have been important for the evening preparations, only one thing was truly necessary and Mary had *chosen* it. She was surrendered. She desired Jesus above all else. I love her story, which we discuss more in later chapters.

HOW TO LIVE SURRENDERED

> *I have been crucified with Christ and I no longer live, but Christ lives in me. The life I now live in the body, I live by faith in the Son of God, who loved me and gave himself for me. —*Galatians 2:20

So, how do we live a life of surrender in our day-to-day routine? It's simpler than it may seem. Of course, our tendency is to overcomplicate matters, but please, for just a moment allow your mind to be open to the simplicity of living a surrendered life daily. Remember, you picked up this book because it's called *Created for the Impossible*.

There is something inside you that hungers to break through those hindering thoughts so you can believe what God says about you, thus stepping into the realm of the impossible with Him! He thinks you can do anything! He knows it because it's His spirit alive and active inside of you. In your weakness, He is made strong in you! So here we go…

You can live a life of total surrender being led by the Spirit of God inside you in your day-to-day living by simply saying, "Yes." That's it. You say *yes. Yes* to whatever the Holy Spirit would lead you to do, or say, or not do, or not say in your day. Period.

God has a plan for the world, friend, and it involves you! He is simply looking for willing vessels. People whose hearts would cooperate with His leading by saying, *"Yes, Lord."* For people who will posture themselves as a willing, open, usable vessel, not worried about what people around them might say or think but who are abandoned to the nudging of the Holy Spirit.

"I am a willing vessel."

"I am a tool! Use me God!"

He's scanning the earth searching for people who will yield their hearts in total surrender relinquishing the reins of their life over to His Spirit.

"Nevertheless, not my will, but Yours be done, God."

My Daughter's Story

There are so many hurting people around us in our daily lives. God desires for His children to partner with His plan and *be* His hands and feet in the earth. For some, this involves going on mission trips to other countries and preaching the good news of the gospel to the poor. For others, this may involve you simply asking God to use you in your daily life to reach the lost, broken, and poor in spirit in the world around you.

When my daughter was nearly four years old, she began what my husband Donovan and I refer to as her "Ministry of Hugs." We would be at the grocery store or the mall and she would tug on my shirt with urgency saying, "Mommy! See that lady over there? I *need* to hug her!" The first time she did this, I was a bit reluctant. I thought about all the mommy "do's" and "don'ts," but staring up at me were these piercing crystal-blue eyes sparkling with pure, authentic *Jesus* compassion. How could I deny that? Before the words "*OK, honey…*" could leave my lips, she was already off and running! I did my best to warn the unsuspecting hug recipient that she was coming but she was so quick I often didn't get to them before her.

It was truly a remarkable sight to see. For some reason she was usually drawn to the ones I considered to be the grumpiest, most "unlikely to receive" individuals. But after she was done with them and I could express, *"I'm so sorry…she just really wanted to hug you,"* I would watch as their once cold, standoffish demeanor shifted to one of, well shock, yes, but also warmth. It was then I realized, she was hugging the life back into people! She was fulfilling the mandate on her life to, like Jesus, bind up the brokenhearted and set the captives free! Her compassion broke through the walls they had built up around their hearts and I got to witness as the love of Jesus went crashing in!

Needless to say, my daughter inspires me to love people more and to not hesitate in sharing the light and love of Jesus in my everyday life. We never know just how we can impact the world around us but the more we posture ourselves as available, willing vessels, the more God will work through us.

As God becomes more and more real to you, living surrendered becomes a beautiful choice you joyfully make each and every day. There's anticipation in the journey ahead knowing that God is going to lead our steps and speak through us, delivering a message of hope, freedom and life to the people around us in our everyday routines.

This hope is a strong and trustworthy anchor for our souls.
It leads us through the curtain into God's inner sanctuary.
—Hebrews 6:19 NLT

BINDING UP THE BROKENHEARTED

The Spirit of the Sovereign LORD is upon me, for the
LORD has anointed me to bring good news to the poor. He
has sent me to comfort the brokenhearted and to proclaim
that captives will be released and prisoners will be freed.
—Isaiah 61:1 NLT

One Saturday morning, my daughter and I were on our way to dance class (*hers, not mine…*) when, by some miracle we were actually running a bit *early*! So, I decided it would be a good time to fill up my near-empty gas tank with fuel. We pulled into the gas station a few blocks from her dance studio and as I was pumping gas I noticed a man sitting against the dumpster in the grass. He had a cigar in one hand and sat with his head leaning back against the dumpster. I immediately noticed his discouraged, broken demeanor and the first thought that jumped in my spirit was, "*I wonder if anyone has prayed with him yet today.*" It wasn't even nine in the morning so I thought this was a strange question…but when I looked at him again, I knew in my heart that this was a very important question to ask.

As I finished pumping the gas, I leaned into my daughter's window. I saw that we still had five minutes before her dance class started. I said to her, "Jenessa, do you see that man over there?" Leaning her head out the window she said with a sincere tone, "Yes." I looked in her eyes and said, "Sweetie, I wonder if anyone has prayed with him yet today." She replied, "I don't know." I asked, "Do you suppose we should go find out?" Before I could even finish asking the question, she was already trying to unbuckle her seatbelt.

So off we went. Hand in hand with my little four-year-old ballerina, we approached the dumpster where this precious man sat, cigar in one hand, beer can in the other.

Smiling we said to him, "Hello sir. We were just getting gas and we saw you over here and we wondered, has anyone prayed with you yet today?" Stunned he replied with a timid, "Well, no…" I said, "Would it be OK if we prayed with you?" "Sure," he said. And with that we were kneeling beside him. He sat his beer can down and I held his free hand. As we prayed, my sweet daughter was busy building a little pile of leaves there next to us. I never try to make her do anything in particular…if she felt she needed to build a leaf pile then by all means, build away, my dear! She was safe by my side so that's what mattered most to my mama heart at this point.

As we prayed, I asked the man if he had a relationship with Jesus. I remembered before we had started praying he had mentioned something about not being able to get the darkness to leave him alone. So, we ended up leading our new friend in a prayer of salvation! Right there next to the dumpster, our new friend began to declare Jesus as Lord of His life and surrendered His heart over to God completely! It was truly phenomenal! I never know how these prayers are going to go and when I pray with people on the fly like that I don't go into it with a plan…just an open heart and sensitivity to the moving of the Spirit. After all, the Spirit only communicates what He hears directly from the Father (see John 16:13). What could be better?

When we were done praying, I acknowledged my sweet daughter's little leaf pile she had built with such purpose and focus. We thanked him for letting us pray with him, blessed him, and were on our way. We were halfway to the car when Jenessa stopped abruptly, looked up at me, and with that sparkle of compassion in her eye she said, "Mommy! I *need* to hug our friend!" I hesitated for a moment as I pictured the cigar, the beer, and the green gunk I had noticed near his eye. Looking at my little ballerina adorned in delicate pastel pinks and purples, I didn't know what to do. But before I could put too much *thought* into it, she tugged on my hand and said with fervency, "Mommy, *please!* I *need* to hug him..." She must know my "yes" body language well because my "OK, Sweetie" barely escaped my lips before she took off running to him.

I turned around and before I could say a word to warn him she leapt into his lap flinging her arms around his neck. His arms wrapped around her back—cigar and all. She gave him one final squeeze and then jumped up joyfully smiling and waving goodbye as she returned to my side and took my hand.

Time seemed to stop as I stood there in the middle of the gas station lot and locked eyes with our friend. With my daughter now by my side with her hand in mine, I watched as tears flooded his eyes. All we could do was smile at each other and nod—understanding that something indescribable had just taken place. The pure presence of God was near tangible around us. My heart is pounding in my chest as I recall this powerful day. God truly longs to use us, His children, flaws and all, to participate in Jesus' mission to bind up the brokenhearted and set the captives free. *If we'll only let Him....*

As we drove away, I watched through my window as our new friend, who just moments ago slouched next to the dumpster defeated and broken, slowly lifted his gaze to the heavens as the peace of God came flooding over Him. I watched as a joy-filled smile crossed his face while he breathed in deeply, closed his eyes, and then exhaled. The breath of God. Peace. This man, Russ, didn't realize that sitting by the dumpster that day was the very place of encounter with His Heavenly Father. *Thank you Lord.*

> I see Jesus in every human being. I say to myself, this is hungry Jesus, I must feed him. This is sick Jesus. This one has leprosy or gangrene; I must wash him and tend to him. I serve because I love Jesus. —Mother Teresa

God drew near to Russ that day and He used my daughter and me as His hands and feet to bring hope to a once-hopeless soul. God trusted Jenessa and me with this brokenhearted one because He knew He could. What an honor, friend—to know that God can trust you with the lost and hurting souls around you? To me there is no greater honor than to know that God sees me as a vessel surrendered enough to be able to use me in even the most undesirable of situations.

I want to encourage you today, friend. If you've been feeling that God has more for you, perhaps He is awaiting a fresh moment of surrender from you. Perhaps that *more* you are seeking comes as you posture yourself in this *"Yes, Lord"* position. Laying down your pride, your own ambitions, and goals, and simply saying to the Father, "I trust you, God, so I surrender all that I am—mind, will and emotions—to you. Use me as your available, willing vessel to reach those who are lost and hurting around me. Help me to see Jesus in everyone! I am yours."

Let's break through those hindering thoughts like *it's too complicated, what can I possibly do for the Kingdom, I'll never be perfect...* and simply embrace that God sees you as His ambassador on the earth! You represent your Father, friend! You've got a mission and if you'll simply surrender your doubt, fear, guilt, worry, everything to Him, laying it all at the feet of Jesus, He'll begin to use your ordinary life in extraordinary ways for His Kingdom! Never underestimate the power of even *one* changed heart! That is the greatest miracle of all—the way Jesus can change a heart and restore a life!

God wants to use you, friend. Simply say *yes* today to His call. As you do this, He will begin to lead you into a life of fearless obedience. Obedience that has you step out of the boat you are in and when your foot lands on what shouldn't be a firm foundation, it somehow is. Because it's the impossible realm of the Kingdom of God, where His children are beckoned to walk.

Jesus walks on water and He's calling out to you to join Him... *will you?*

What is He saying to you?

Chapter 4

FEARLESS OBEDIENCE: LIVING LIFE OUTSIDE THE BOAT

Obedience is better than sacrifice.
—1 Samuel 15:22 nlt

Love for God launches us into our obedience to Him and stirs up the love we have for others. Our love for people springs from our relationship with the Father. We love Him so deeply that we begin to love what He loves, and what He loves is His creation! His most beloved creation is *you*! So now, we begin seeing the world around us through the lens of perfect love, and fear has no place!

> *There is no fear in love. But perfect love drives out fear, because fear has to do with punishment. The one who fears is not made perfect in love.* —1 John 4:18

I pray this book encourages you to dive into the heart of God where you fall madly in love with Him. That your relationship with Him grows personal and intimate as you begin to see yourself the way God sees you and come to know His fierce love for you. Your love for

Him and His love for you should shine a new light on the way you love others. His voice and His leading should compel you in reaching out to people. Because it's His perfect love that causes your lens to change, so you see people the way God sees them, with compassion and mercy.

Let His love be the launching pad propelling you into greater obedience and increased faith as your perspective continues to shift. Obligation should have no place in our hearts because obligation is rooted in religion. Obedience is rooted in love. God does not *obligate* us. He empowers us to *choose* what is right.

OBEDIENCE, GREAT FAITH, AND GREAT LOVE DEMONSTRATED

Tears streamed down my face as I finally closed the book I had been reading for a couple of weeks. *I was finished*! I knew this book was one that I needed in this season of my life. It's called *The Noticer Returns* and is written by one of my heroes, Andy Andrews. Andy is an inspiration for many reasons. He has a powerful testimony of being homeless, living under the pier in Orange Beach, AL. after both of his parents had died when he was young. His story about how he turned his life around is inspiring to say the least. He is also the only author who has managed to grab my husband's attention enough for him to read through an entire book, *The Noticer*, in just two sittings! My husband is one to never finish a book, and if he does, it's after months and months of picking away at it.

I didn't know why I was drawn to reading this book as I was in the throes of writing my own book at the time. But I just knew, I needed to read it. Ironically, in it Mr. Andrews weaves into the narrative how he was in the midst of writing one of his books and was desperate for inspiration.

Closing the book for the last time, I sat in the quiet solitude of my grandparents' back patio. The birds were chirping joyful melodies and the leaves rustled gently in the light Florida breeze. Tears began streaming down my face as I closed my eyes and listened as the Holy Spirit whispered a simple, yet life-altering, statement, "When you are obedient and step out in faith, it's as though you are wrapping your arms around *Me* and saying, *'I love you.'*"

Not wanting to move, I let that sink in. I began pondering what God has called me to do in this particular season—*write my book.* And I recalled the question He asked me the other night at church as I worshiped, *"Are you writing this book because you love Me?"* I remembered lifting my gaze toward Heaven with tears streaming down my face, which seems to happen a lot, I know. It was in that moment that I allowed any other motive or desire to simply fall away as I uttered these words from my heart, *"Yes, Lord. I am writing the book because I love you. Purely and simply—I love you so I am writing this book."* I then had a vision of a nut—yes, *a nut.* In the center of the nut is the meat and on the outside is the shell. As I allowed any motive or desire that wasn't in line with God's to fall away, it was as though the shell had been cracked and fell off the nut, revealing the center, or the meat— the *purpose,* if you will. Writing this book is an act of worship to the Father. It's what He has called and commissioned me to do in this season. So I'm being obedient. And I'm obeying because I love Him!

How often do we say to the Lord, *"I love you Lord."* Yet we hesitate when He asks us to do something for Him. While we may be genuinely sincere in our proclamation of love for Him, He's asking us for more than mere words. He's looking for our obedience.

Do not merely listen to the word, and so deceive yourselves. Do what it says. Anyone who listens to the word but does not do what it says is like someone who looks at his face in a mirror and, after looking at himself, goes away and immediately forgets what he looks like. But whoever looks intently into the perfect law that gives freedom, and continues in it—not forgetting what they have heard,

but doing it—they will be blessed in what they do.
—James 1:22-25

Even seemingly simple things like hugging a stranger at the grocery store, as my daughter loves to do, or speaking a word of encouragement to someone at a restaurant when we feel that inner nudge to do so, are very important. Listen friend, the ministry of the Holy Spirit here on earth, in our hearts, is to get us to do what Jesus would do if He were walking the earth today. Do you think that if Jesus were in the grocery store and sensed that a person was hurting He would look the other way? Of course not! He would go to them and offer them encouragement, prayer, and anything else they needed and/or He felt in His spirit to do.

It's simple. The Holy Spirit empowers us to be like Jesus. Jesus had no fear because His trust in God was greater. Jesus' love for the Father caused Him to believe every word from the Father, which empowered Him to live His life on earth in fearless obedience. Whether in the midst of a storm or in the presence of darkness, Jesus was fearless! *And you can be too, friend*!

DAVID'S STORY

The LORD has sought out a man after his own heart and appointed him ruler of his people. —1 Samuel 13:14

Reading the story of David, we see how God chose him to be king because he was deemed *"a man after His own heart."* David had a pure heart. Before he was appointed king, David gained favor in the kingdom as a mighty warrior. David was triumphant over the giant, Goliath, who no one could defeat before him. But as David's popularity grew, Saul's heart began to harden more and more, filling with jealousy, anger, and pride.

Saul was very angry; this refrain displeased him greatly. "They have credited David with tens of thousands," he thought, "but me with only thousands. What more can he get but the kingdom?" And from that time on Saul kept a close eye on David. —1 Samuel 18:8-9

Several chapters of First Samuel describe Saul's pursuit to kill David. With relentless furry, Saul chased David for many, many years. I believe that Saul's pursuit of David is a reflection of pride's pursuit of the pure hearted.

There is a giant out there today and the Body of Christ has been trying to see its influence dissolved for many years. I believe that giant is today's worldly culture and the *power* it has to influence a generation. *But that can change with just one stone…*

*Goliath stood and shouted to the ranks of Israel, "Why do you come out and line up for battle? Am I not a Philistine, and are you not the **servants of Saul?** Choose a man and have him come down to me. If he is able to fight and kill me, we will become your subjects; but if I overcome him and kill him, you will become our subjects and serve us." Then the Philistine said, "This day I defy the armies of Israel! Give me a man and let us fight each other." On hearing the Philistine's words, Saul and all the Israelites were dismayed and terrified. —1 Samuel 17:8-11*

The seed of deception had been planted through Goliath's words as he declared to God's people that they were nothing more than mere "servants of *Saul.*" This one lie sowed a seed of deception into the hearts of the Israelites, declaring that they were nothing special, just mere servants of king Saul. As the men believed the lie and the narrative roaring over them by this intimidator, their perspective shifted from their true power source—*God Almighty*—and they began to see themselves as common soldiers fighting for their earthly king instead of mighty warriors fighting for Almighty God. *How could they defeat such a giant?* Suddenly Goliath wasn't just a giant in the physical, but a giant in their minds as well. His taunts provoked fear. The more they believed he couldn't be defeated, the more the fear grew. They had elevated Goliath based on his physical appearance and his threats. One by one they fled in fear, trading their confidence in God Almighty for their fear of man.

Fear caused them to flee from the mantle on their life as warriors in God's army!

Wow, friend! How often do we do the same thing in our day-to-day life? It's as though the one who speaks the loudest into our identity is the one we believe! Whichever voice we choose to listen to most, will be the one with the greatest influence. Suddenly, before we know it, we are trading our confidence in God for our fear of man. We forfeit the reality of our identity as a child of God for the identity we see the world portraying around us as nothing more than *mere men/women. "Who am I? I'm nothing special..."* we find ourselves thinking.

This challenges our obedience, leading us into a tough choice— do we ignore the lies and obey God or do we believe the lies and, for fear, flee from the destiny God is leading us into because there is a giant in our way?

Listen friend, being a child of God and confident in Christ doesn't mean we walk around in arrogance, that is what the world does and it's false because it means putting your confidence in yourself. No, being a strong, confident child of God means we walk in boldness, authority, and *meekness* because our confidence is in God. You have the Spirit of God inside you! He is greater than any giant, any mountain, and any other obstacle in your path!

Just as Goliath mocked and intimidated the Israelites at the battle line, so culture has mocked and tried to intimate the children of God from crossing the threshold of fear and rising up in the boldness and authority we inherit as heirs of the Kingdom of God. God is looking for those who will come forward, fearlessly approaching the battle line armed with truth, ready to take on whatever stands in their path!

And just as David—a mere shepherd boy who the world dis-qualified—came forward in boldness to conquer that which was intimidating and seemed impossible to overcome, so God is raising up the pure of heart to go boldly forward in obedience, crossing furi-ously over the threshold of fear, compelled by love, armed with truth, and fueled by faith!

APPROACHING THE BATTLE LINE

In First Samuel 17:22, we see David leaving his flock to bring sup-plies for his brothers at the battlefield. While there, he went to check on his brothers and overheard the threats and scoffs spewing from the giant Philistine man.

> *David left his things with the keeper of supplies, ran to the battle lines and asked his brothers how they were. As he was talking with them, Goliath, the Philistine cham-pion from Gath, stepped out from his lines and shouted his usual defiance, and David heard it. Whenever the Isra-elites saw the man, they all fled from him in great fear.*
> —1 Samuel 17:22-24

I believe that just as David was drawn to the battle line and to the very thing intimidating and mocking the armies of God, so God is drawing *you* to be a voice willing to speak up for truth in a generation drowning in the lies, scoffs, and mockery of our worldly culture. Let's take a look at the rest of the story,

> *Now the Israelites had been saying, "Do you see how this man keeps coming out? He comes out to defy Israel. The king will give great wealth to the man who kills him. He will also give him his daughter in marriage and will exempt his family from taxes in Israel.*
> *David asked the men standing near him, "What will be done for the man who kills this Philistine and removes*

this disgrace from Israel? **Who is this uncircumcised Philistine that he should defy the armies of the living God?"**

They repeated to him what they had been saying and told him, "This is what will be done for the man who kills him."

When Eliab, David's oldest brother, heard him speaking with the men, he burned with anger at him and asked, "Why have you come down here? And with whom did you leave those few sheep in the wilderness? I know how conceited you are and how wicked your heart is; you came down only to watch the battle."

"Now what have I done?" said David. "Can't I even speak?" He then turned away to someone else and brought up the same matter, and the men answered him as before. What David said was overheard and reported to Saul, and Saul sent for him. —1 Samuel 17:25-31

Here we see David's own brother attempting to silence his voice. Many times it is those closest to us who misunderstand us most. We can't allow anyone or anything to halt or hinder our obedience to God. David is inspiring to me for many reasons, one of which is the way he ignored the lies, from the scoffing giant and even his own brother. David's heart belonged to God and he knew who he was as a result! *David believed what God said about him.*

Another important facet to note is how David couldn't fathom the mockery coming out of the mouth of Goliath. In verse 26, David acknowledges that Goliath is mocking the "armies of the *living God.*" This is inconceivable to David. His perspective is right on point, whereas those in the army apparently forgot *whom* they were fighting for! I believe their perspective shifted in the midst of all the mockery! While they had originally assembled as the army of God, the constant scoffs from the enemy thwarted their perspective of who they were and who God was.

> *David said to Saul, "Let no one lose heart on account of this Philistine; your servant will go and fight him."*
>
> *Saul replied, "You are not able to go out against this Philistine and fight him; you are only a young man, and he has been a warrior from his youth."*
>
> *But David said to Saul, "Your servant has been keeping his father's sheep. When a lion or a bear came and carried off a sheep from the flock, I went after it, struck it and rescued the sheep from its mouth. When it turned on me, I seized it by its hair, struck it and killed it. Your servant has killed both the lion and the bear; this uncircumcised Philistine will be like one of them, because he has defied the armies of the living God. The Lord who rescued me from the paw of the lion and the paw of the bear will rescue me from the hand of this Philistine." Saul said to David, "Go, and the Lord be with you."*
>
> *Then Saul dressed David in his own tunic. He put a coat of armor on him and a bronze helmet on his head. David fastened on his sword over the tunic and tried walking around, because he was not used to them.*
>
> *"I cannot go in these," he said to Saul, "because I am not used to them." So he took them off. Then he took his staff in his hand, chose five smooth stones from the stream, put them in the pouch of his shepherd's bag and, with his sling in his hand, approached the Philistine.* —1 Samuel 17:32-40

David approached the battle line wearing nothing more than his old tunic. He didn't wear the armor man offered; he had on the whole armor of God! Though no one could see it in the natural, it was the only thing David needed to defeat the giant! He wore the belt of truth and the breastplate of righteousness. He had on the shoes of peace as He walked in the peace of God to that battle line knowing *Who* would be fighting through him to defeat the accuser before him. Unlike the rest of the army, David knew whom he was fighting for and who would be empowering him.

This passage also reflects the reason God saw David as a man after his own heart. David was a shepherd tending to the sheep. When a bear or a lion came to devour just one of the sheep, David didn't allow it! He pursued the bear and the lion rescuing the *one* sheep from its mouth! David's heart in action to rescue the one sheep is one of the reasons why he was regarded as a man after God's heart. You are the *one* sheep God rescues! He snatches you from the very mouth of the enemy! By the blood of His Son He rescues you from the teeth of the enemy, ripping you from his clenched jaw, setting you atop the path He marked out for you before the very foundations of the world were formed!

> *We all, like sheep, have gone astray, each of us has turned to our own way; and the Lord has laid on him the iniquity of us all. He was oppressed and afflicted, yet he did not open his mouth; he was led like a lamb to the slaughter, and as a sheep before its shearers is silent, so he did not open his mouth.* —Isaiah 53:6-7

Friend, Jesus willingly placed Himself within the clench of death so that once and for all you would be freed from the teeth of the enemy. Now, through Christ Jesus you are free! You do not need to fear the enemy's bite because he has no power and no hold over you! Just as David freed his sheep from the jaw of the enemy, so your Heavenly Father has freed you! He gave up His own life through His Son, placing Himself in death's hold so that He could demolish that grip once and for all, *for you*...because He loves you.

The enemy is all talk, friend! His lies, his accusations, they are just that—lies and accusations! Their only power exists from believing the lie—deny the lie and nullify its power! The enemy may snarl his ugly teeth at you but, as the saying goes, he's all bark and no bite! The enemy has grown accustomed to having power over people. But now, you can stop him from having power over you! You are a redeemed child of God! The enemy can only have power over you if you allow him. He is fueled by your doubt, your fear, and/or your unbelief. The truth of the matter is you have been given authority and power through Christ Jesus who took up residence inside of you the moment you surrendered your life to Him and were born again.

Let me state this in another way to further illustrate the point so you really, truly, and deeply get it today. The enemy has no authentic power! He has no grip! Jesus triumphed over satan on the cross! Now, through the resurrection power of Christ, death has lost its sting (see 1 Cor. 15:55)! All authority was given to Jesus, which He gives to you. Your power source lives inside you! *Jesus!* So don't relinquish any of your power and authority to feed the lies of the devil. We only give the lie power when we believe it! But if you believe what God says about you instead, and who He says you are, then you'll starve out the lies and feed the Spirit of Truth within you. Just as a wall will crumble from an explosion so will lies crumble from the explosion of truth!

Speak truth over yourself, believe in your heart, and allow the identity God speaks over you to triumph! Remember, He thinks you can do anything. He really, *really* does.

THE PURE HEART SLAYS THE GIANT

As David approached the battle line in his shepherd clothes with his staff and his stone, Goliath attempted to mock and intimidate him as he did the rest of the army. But his lies didn't matter to David because David knew *whom* he was fighting for and *who* was fighting the battle through him,

Meanwhile, the Philistine, with his shield bearer in front of him kept coming closer to David. He looked David over and saw that he was little more than a boy, glowing with health and handsome, and he despised him. He said to David, "Am I a dog, that you come at me with sticks?" And the Philistine cursed David by his gods. "Come here," he said, "and I'll give your flesh to the birds and the wild animals!"

David said to the Philistine, "You come against me with sword and spear and javelin, but I come against you in the name of the Lord Almighty, the God of the armies of Israel, whom you have defied. This day the Lord will deliver you into my hands, and I'll strike you down and cut off your head. This very day I will give the carcasses of the Philistine army to the birds and the wild animals, and the whole world will know that there is a God in Israel. All those gathered here will know that it is not by sword or spear that the Lord saves; for the battle is the Lord's, and he will give all of you into our hands."

As the Philistine moved closer to attack him, David ran quickly toward the battle line to meet him. Reaching into his bag and taking out a stone, he slung it and struck the Philistine on the forehead. The stone sank into his forehead, and he fell facedown on the ground.

So David triumphed over the Philistine with a sling and a stone; without a sword in his hand he struck down the Philistine and killed him. —1 Samuel 17:41-50

Through David's courage and obedience, the whole of Israel's army was successful in battle and conquered the rest of the Philistine army. It's interesting how it only took *one* to intimidate an entire army. One who was bold enough to mock and stir up fear in the hearts of the soldiers. And so, it took just one who was courageous enough to defeat him. Lies are empty but truth comes with power and authority! Rise up in truth as David did by putting your hope and confidence in the Lord your God and you will be victorious in any battle, facing any giant!

David took simple steps of faith. He didn't have an agenda. He just walked in the power of the Lord and was faithfully and fearlessly obedient.

If God is for us who can be against us? —Romans 8:31

Through this story God has been teaching me about the solution to the influence of today's culture—*a pure heart.* What does that look like? I believe the smooth stone that David picked up from the stream and thrust at the arrogant giant before him represents the pure heart. The thrust of the pure heart comes from the Spirit of the living God inside us. We have the power! We have the authority! Because we have Jesus in us!

David walked in fearless obedience because of who God is. He didn't put on man's armor to slay the giant, which I also believe represents the way things have been done before—*the world's way.* He trusted God's way and through trust and a pure heart he slayed the very thing that armies before him had tried and failed to overcome. David knew he was fighting for God and thus knew without a doubt that God would go before him—*he wasn't alone.*

Friend, we are living in a time where the antidote to the downfall of our world is the pure heart. The pure heart of those who will rise up in fearless obedience knowing they are part of the Lord's army. Just as the stone was smoothed of all its sharp edges and rough places in the stream, so our heart will be purified and smoothed out in the living water through the blood of Jesus. His blood is the only thing that purifies and cleanses the heart! So, as believers who are washed in the blood of Jesus begin to lay down human agenda and begin to rise up in response to the call of God on our lives, trusting Him with abandon, fearlessly obedient to the call of God in our life, we will begin to see the giant of culture's influence on our churches, schools, medical systems, and more begin to crumble.

> *But now, this is what the Lord says…"Do not fear, for I have redeemed you; I have summoned you by name; you are mine. When you pass through the waters, I will be with you; and when you pass through the rivers, they will not sweep over you. When you walk through the fire, you will not be burned; the flames will not set you ablaze. For I am the Lord your God, the Holy One of Israel, your Savior."*
> —Isaiah 43:1-3

David's fearlessness, which led to his obedience, was a result of his deep trust in God and his trust flowed from his love for God.

God is looking for the pure of heart and He longs for your love. He longs for you to trust Him enough that you'll take just one faith step at a time into your destiny. One step is all it takes. Likewise, each step you refuse to take forward in obedience can get you out of balance and alignment with God. Disobedience interrupts your destiny and hinders your progress. Don't underestimate the power of each step. There is no step too small to take because each seemingly small step in obedience represents a giant leap forward into your destiny. Which will you choose today, friend—moving forward or holding back? As shared in Chapter 3, God is looking for your willing heart. Fearless obedience is you choosing to move past your fear in order to obey. God desires obedience over sacrifice.

PETER'S STORY

> *Then Peter got down out of the boat, walked on the water and came toward Jesus. But when he saw the wind, he was afraid and, beginning to sink, cried out, "Lord, save me!" Immediately Jesus reached out his hand and caught him. "You of little faith," he said, "why did you doubt?"*
> —Matthew 14:29-31

Here we have Peter responding to Jesus by stepping out of the boat and onto the waters with Jesus. Peter's love for Jesus fueled his trust, and his trust caused him to step out of the boat and fearlessly walk out onto the unknown, obeying the One calling him out of the boat. But interestingly in this story we see the reverse begin to happen as well, *fearlessness* propelled him and *fearfulness* caused him to sink,

> *Shortly before dawn Jesus went out to them, walking on the lake. When the disciples saw him walking on the lake, they were terrified. "It's a ghost," they said, and cried out in fear.*
>
> *But Jesus immediately said to them: "Take courage! It is I. Don't be afraid."*
>
> *"Lord, if it's you," Peter replied, "tell me to come to you on the water."*
>
> *"Come," he said.*
>
> *Then Peter got down out of the boat, walked on the water and came toward Jesus. But when he saw the wind, he was afraid and, beginning to sink, cried out, "Lord, save me!"*
>
> *Immediately Jesus reached out his hand and caught him. "You of little faith," he said, "why did you doubt?"*
>
> *And when they climbed into the boat, the wind died down. Then those who were in the boat worshiped him, saying, "Truly you are the Son of God."* —Matthew 14:25-33

There is just something about the word "*come*" when released from the mouth of our Savior! Peter needed to know that it was Jesus out there on the water so he asks Him, "Lord if it's you tell me to come to you on the water." Much like the initial call Peter heard from the Lord that incredible day when Jesus says, *"Come, follow me"* (Matt. 4:19). Something about His tone...it wasn't a suggestion, it was a command for Peter to "*Come.*" Everything inside of Peter must have been drawn to that mandate as one end of a magnet is drawn to another. Something about His voice brought a security Peter had never known before. It must have, because Peter willingly walked away from everything he had worked for in his life.

Now in this passage we see Peter requesting that same mandate, "Lord, if that's you, tell me to come to you." So Jesus says, *"Come."* And Peter responds. He lays down His fear in order to obey. He chooses to step out of the boat atop the impossible because the Lord had called him out, and thus empowered him to leave everything that once brought comfort. This felt familiar…only Jesus could accomplish this. Peter's love for Jesus compelled him to trust, and his trust birthed fearlessness, which led to his obedience. But the moment Peter began to *see* the wind, he began to fear and his fear caused him to doubt, which resulted in him sinking.

But let's look at what Jesus did as Peter began to sink from doubt—Jesus reached out His hand and caught him! He then rebuked his unbelief and questioned his doubt. The moment they were back in the boat—back in what was comfortable—the wind, which caused fear and doubt, died down.

What a message here, friend! This was a divine setup for Peter. Jesus created an opportunity for Peter to fearlessly obey. Regardless of circumstance, God wants our trust! It's easy to trust Him when the wind isn't raging around us, but what about those stormy seasons of life? Will you trust Him then? When you can't see Him *or* hear Him, but you can feel Him drawing you—what will you choose to do? *Trust, or doubt?*

What is God asking of you in this particular season of your life? What seemingly simple faith step is He wooing you to take? Don't underestimate the power in each step, friend! It was in one step that David obeyed the Lord. It was in just one step that Peter walked on water. One faith step at a time is all God is looking for in you. Will you listen? Will you choose to believe what God says about you versus the narrative the enemy tries to speak into your life? God thinks you can do anything, friend. He knows it!

He's calling you now to step out into the unknown with Him, and with that call comes authority, boldness, courage, and power— everything you need to fulfill the call of God on your life. It's going to be wild! It's an adventure of a lifetime! It's your faith journey with Jesus. *Just you and Him…hand in hand.*

Your journey might look different than mine but I can tell you this—it doesn't come with a map! You are currently writing the map with your life so that others might come after you and begin where you leave off. Your children will be able to look back and see each mile marker you've crossed and each step you took. You are leaving a legacy of faith for future generations! This is what it means to be a "history maker." You are making history right now with your life, friend. Keep on going. Never stop. And don't underestimate small beginnings. Trust the Lord, *He made a way for you.*

> *Trust in the Lord with all your heart and lean not on your own understanding; in all your ways acknowledge Him, and He shall direct your paths.* —Proverbs 3:5-6 NKJV

What is He saying to you?

_____

_____

_____

_____

_____

_____

_____

_____

_____

_____

Chapter 5

HE MADE A WAY FOR YOU

But God demonstrates his own love for us in this:
While we were still sinners, Christ died for us.
—ROMANS 5:8

The number *five*, as in *Chapter* 5, is the number of grace. And that's precisely what this chapter is about: God's amazing grace for humanity that He sent His beloved Son into the world to save the world (see John 3:16–17), not condemn it as some would like to believe. Jesus' life beautifully demonstrates the reality of God's plan, His nature, and His unsearchable love for us, which was to offer up His heart to humanity, and not His wrath or condemnation. Jesus was often seen shielding those whom man had deemed worthy of condemnation with His robe of righteousness.

If you'll recall from the Introduction, in the vision I had of Jesus taking me by the hand and walking me through moments of *His*-story, there was the story of the woman caught in adultery from John Chapter 7 and 8. In my vision, Jesus had run to shield her with His arms. The dust was stirred up by His fierce, swift movement as He reached her just in time to cover her.

After writing down this vision, I sought it out in Scripture. I had this lingering question in my spirit: *Did He really run to protect her from the stones?* Reading through the Scriptures, we see the testimony of this moment in the Bible depicts Jesus as kneeling down on the ground writing in the sand.

> *At dawn he appeared again in the temple courts, where all the people gathered around him, and he sat down to teach them. The teachers of the law and the Pharisees brought in a woman caught in adultery. They made her stand before the group and said to Jesus, "Teacher, this woman was caught in the act of adultery. In the Law Moses commanded us to stone such women. Now what do you say?" They were using this question as a trap, in order to have a basis for accusing him.*
>
> *But Jesus bent down and started to write on the ground with his finger. When they kept on questioning him, he straightened up and said to them, "Let any one of you who is without sin be the first to throw a stone at her." Again he stooped down and wrote on the ground.*
>
> *At this, those who heard began to go away one at a time, the older ones first, until only Jesus was left, with the woman still standing there. Jesus straightened up and asked her, "Woman, where are they? Has no one condemned you?"*
>
> *"No one, sir," she said.*
>
> *"Then neither do I condemn you," Jesus declared. "Go now and leave your life of sin."* —John 8:2-11

I believe the way the Lord showed it to me was significant, pertaining to the urgency of Jesus' heart to shield her. Essentially, He did just that with His Words and I believe His Words provided her with the covering she needed. His Words brought forth hope, they spoke correction to her accusers, and they provided salvation to the woman.

In the vision, she had been thrown before Him and He shielded her with His robe. I believe this represents His robe of righteousness that He covers each and every one of us in through grace. *"Righteous,"* is what Jesus declares over us through His blood! No longer do we cower in shame but we rise up boldly shining through His grace on our life. This is how we demonstrate our belief in what He did for us, as well as our acceptance of this amazing gift of salvation. Jesus didn't die so that we would continue carrying our heavy load of guilt, worry, grief, shame, and unforgiveness. *No!* Jesus died to free us by His blood. He carried our load of guilt, worry, grief, shame, and unforgiveness upon Himself the day He died on the cross, freeing us once and for all! Our heavy load was crucified with Christ. God deeply desires that you give Him honor by accepting what He did and allowing Christ to shine brightly through you each and every day!

Reflecting Jesus as a mirror, which we discuss more in later chapters, is a beautiful way of showing Christ to the lost and broken world around you! You are essentially saying, "Thank you Jesus for the price you paid for me on the cross," as you allow the guilt, the worry, and the shame to fall off of you. As you allow the old to pass away and step into the new creation Jesus died for you to become, you are giving honor to the Son for the price He paid on the cross. This is a beautiful expression of your acceptance of Jesus and your gratitude to the Father for sending the Son. Think about it, what better way can you demonstrate your gratitude than by fully embracing who He died for you to become—*a new creation in Christ, a child of God.*

WHEN THE CROSS BECAME REAL TO ME

I was born again at four years old in the big brown chair on my daddy's lap. That is how I've always told the story and I can still vividly remember that special moment, having replayed it over and over in my spirit throughout the years of my life. Needless to say, having grown up in the church, when I became an adult I just *assumed* I knew what the cross was all about. I never would have thought otherwise until God used a conference I was preparing for to reveal just how clueless I actually was to the simple, yet profound and powerful truth of the cross.

It was in early 2014 as I was getting ready for my upcoming conference that I could heard the Holy Spirit say to me, *"It's all about the cross, Krissy…it's all about the cross." "OK, Lord"* my heart replied. *"Of course…"* As if to say, "Well yeah, *I know that.*" But as I began to seek Him, spending time in His presence preparing for this conference, I began asking myself a very simple, seemingly obvious question, *"So what is the cross all about, really?"* And I realized the shocking reality was, I didn't *really* know.

This led me on a journey that has forever changed my life and refocused my ministry and message. As I sought Him I realized, if someone asked me to sum up what the cross was all about in as few words as possible, I wasn't sure I could do it! And in just a few short weeks I would have a bunch of hungry women in front of me longing for more of the Lord in their lives. These were mothers, wives, sisters, daughters…and they were taking time out of their busy lives to attend what was at the time my second conference ever. I don't take these things lightly. I was also informed that Teen Challenge was going to be bringing their entire women's center as well, so I was ready to dive into what the Holy Spirit wanted to unveil to my heart about the cross.

My heart's desire when speaking is to make things simple. The Gospel message while beautifully deep is also quite simple. We tend to overcomplicate it all, which can lead to confusion, which, interestingly, is where I found myself at the moment—*confused.*

This was strange for me. The most basic element of Christianity and here I was at a loss for what it all really meant. I had grown up in the church, been to hundreds of services, experienced the presence of God in powerful ways, and had come through a massive revival, yet here I was, just over 30, a mom of two, married for over a decade, in ministry, and was asking myself what seemed the most simple of questions for a *"seasoned"* Christian—*What is the cross really about? How does the cross impact my life today?*

I'll never forget the night the cross became real to me. I was driving home from a prayer meeting. It was dark and the beams of my headlights seemed to dance in the foggy night breeze as I drove. Lost in thought, I began considering the women in the Teen Challenge program. Their *testimonies!* Many of them pulled from the pit of despair and drug addiction, abuse, anger, rage, and yet now, having accepted Christ, they were full of joy. They have peace. They are redeemed! They shine bright with the joy of the Lord. The cross became real to them. They had been forgiven of much and in turn they loved much! As Jesus said in Luke regarding Mary as she poured out her finest perfume upon His feet and washed them with her tears, *"her many sins have been forgiven—as her great love has shown,"* (Luke 7:47).

Thinking through the testimonies I had heard from my friends at Teen Challenge, I began reflecting on my own testimony. I wondered if I lacked zeal and knowledge of the cross because I had known Christ my whole life. Maybe my story didn't pack enough punch, so to speak. Maybe I didn't comprehend the message of the cross enough because I hadn't had it pull me out of the pit as these women had. But in my spirit I knew that wasn't right thinking so I began praying and crying out to God.

"Father, show me the cross! Show me why it's relevant today and how it has shaped my life's testimony! Show me, Father! Please…"

Suddenly a thought so simple yet powerful hit my heart. A thought that spoke to me right where I was in life as a new mom, *"Because of the cross I don't have to feel the weight of 'mommy guilt' anymore. The cross takes all that away."* It sounds so simple I know, but it met me where I was at in this particular stage in my life with a two-year-old son and a three-year-old daughter. I was riddled with "mommy guilt," the fear of failure, the shame of imperfection, and so much more. Suddenly I could see clearly. I could see Jesus there on the cross and all of my life's issues were on Him. All of my guilt (past and present), my shame, my fear, all there upon the perfect Son, the spotless Lamb of God tarnished not by His own doing but by my sin, and the sin of all humanity there on the cross! Everything impure and unclean was heaped upon the innocent Lamb of God. He bore it all upon Himself. All so I could live a life free of these things. *This* I realized was a glimpse at the abundant life Jesus died for, a life free of guilt, shame, sin, fear, anger, and so much more.

I realized in that moment that living this life of freedom and the joy that flows from Jesus is the testimony of the cross in my life. I could see that my testimony carried just as much power as anyone else's because it pointed people to Jesus. It's not the measure of sin we've been freed from that determines the freedom we walk in, it's the measure of the price paid for our sin that establishes our freedom! Out of His love, God gave up His Son to free us once and for all. Whom the Son sets free is free indeed (see John 8:36)!

> *And I am convinced that nothing can ever separate us from God's love. Neither death nor life, neither angels nor demons, neither our fears for today nor our worries about tomorrow—not even the powers of hell can separate us from God's love. No power in the sky above or in the earth below—indeed, nothing in all creation will ever be able to separate us from the love of God that is revealed in Christ Jesus our Lord.* —Romans 8:38-39 NLT

Christ died to free us from the weight and grip of sin, period. So, once I realized what His sacrifice covered, I could rejoice and testify of the power and goodness of God in my life! I can share of the cross and the amazing grace and love of Jesus, that now there is nothing that separates us fro m the love of God. Where there was once a chasm separating me from the Father, that gap has been bridged by the arms of Christ on the cross. We now have full access to the Father through the Son!

There's no comparing our testimonies—each of us has our own story to share. His blood covers our sins, it spares us from death, and it serves as a shield of protection around us. Friend, if you're reading this, then you too have a story to share of the power of the blood of Jesus in your life. You may not even realize it but it's there! Ask the Holy Spirit to show you how the blood of Jesus has protected you, saved you, washed you, covered you, and how it is working through you!

Before you were ever born, a way was made for you to come into the family of God. This plan was made before the foundations of the earth were ever formed (see 1 Pet. 1:20)! Before your first step which led to your first scraped knee and your first kiss leading to your first heartbreak—a way was made for your healing. Before your first sin, a way was made for your cleansing and reconciliation to God. You are born into a remarkable time in *His*-story because the way has been made for you already! You need only believe and receive this beautiful gift from God if you haven't already.

SHIFTING YOUR PERSPECTIVE

God made him who had no sin to be sin for us so that in him we might become the righteousness of God.
—2 Corinthians 5:21

This is such a powerful verse. More powerful than I think we can even comprehend, so we often brush past it. But it really is everything! God made Jesus, who had no sin in Him whatsoever, actually *become* sin so that we—you and me—could *become* the righteousness of God. *What?!?*

Oftentimes for me to really wrap my brain around something this big, I like to think of it in terms that I would describe to my six-year-old…so here it goes.

Sin: this is a verb right? An *action* word. We sin—it's something we either do or we don't do, correct? But in the context of this verse, it's essentially described both as a verb (an action, something we *do)* *and* a noun (a person, place, *thing*)—God made Him who had no *sin* (verb) become *sin* (noun) so that in HIM (*His* righteousness) we might *become* the righteousness of God!

Picture with me if you will sin as a noun instead of an invisible, intangible verb. If I picture sin as a noun, I image a big, black, icky blob with big buggy eyes making faces at me, aiming to intimidate me, or scare me. Yes I know, I know—it sounds silly…but I'm a mom of two small children so this sort of descriptive language comes with the territory, just bear with me, please.

Can you see it?

Now imagine that Jesus, the beautiful spotless Lamb of God, takes upon Himself and fully embodies this big icky blob of sin that represents all the sin of the world, for all time, for all people, past, present, and future. See Him carrying His cross up to Calvary, getting nailed to the cross and then the wrath of God from all eternity past, present, and future pours down on the spotless Lamb who has, in this moment, become engulfed in the big icky sin blob so that He could ensure sin receives its due punishment once and for all time!

It is finished!

It's done!

Hooray! Sin has been defeated and can no longer intimidate, scare, mock, or enslave me! It's power to grip me, bind me, rob me, control me, and kill me has been triumphed over once and finally on the cross! Now, through the blood of Christ, in *Him*, I *become* the righteousness of God! *Whoa!* That's huge!

God didn't redeem the *things* of the world to Himself—He redeemed *people*. So, while sin still exists in this world because it's a fallen world, humanity has a chance to be made clean and righteous before God! And sin can't prevent it from happening anymore! Prior to the cross, sin stained me and made me unclean before God, but now because of the cross, though I may still sin, once I repent of my sin and accept Jesus into my heart, declaring Him Lord and Savior of my life, I am now washed clean by His blood. *For Jesus paid the price. He drank the fullness of the wrath of God, though He begged the Father to take that cup away the night before His crucifixion* (see Luke 22:42). His blood that flowed red washes me white as snow! Now I become spotless in the Father's sight and He remembers my sin no more (see Isa. 43:25)! Halleluiah!

> *I tell you the truth, those who listen to my message and believe in God who sent me have eternal life. They will never be condemned for their sins, but they have already passed from death into life.* —John 5:24 NLT

The cross restored the intimacy available with God for us! It restores us to our position as God's beloved children! We are no longer slaves to sin, fear, and death! We have been bought with a price (see 1 Cor. 6:20) by the precious blood of Jesus! We discuss more about being a child of God in the next chapter as well.

This is good news because it brings the God afar, near! Many of us who consider ourselves to be "Christians" accept and acknowledge God on Sundays or semiannually at Christmas and Easter. We are worshiping God as though He is far off, not interested in our lives. We behave as children who have been sent to boarding school and only engage with our father on holidays. Let me tell you something, this is not the relationship dynamic Jesus died for us to have!

There is *more!*

Our Heavenly Father longs to be near you, friend! He desires fellowship with you. He wants to invest in you. To pour His unfailing, everlasting love *into* you! He's a good Father and longs to say to you, "My child—you're a good son/daughter. I love you and I'm proud of you." He is the God who is close to us and we can be close to Him. The cross restored the fellowship dynamic we are meant to have with the Father as His kids. The implications of believing in the Son are 1) the new life available for the believer (see 2 Cor. 5:17), 2) the opportunity we now have as children of God to go boldly before the Father (see Heb. 4:16), and 3) the authority and power we have over darkness (see Matt. 16:18)!

God thinks you can do anything…

We need to grab hold of this and allow it to impact our everyday lives! When we are experiencing hell on earth, we can draw on Jesus and access the Father in our home, car, even in the waiting room of the doctor's office. When we go through tragedy in life, we need to have the cross so rooted in us that we understand He is right there for us. He releases Heaven in our midst so we can experience peace even in the midst of our pain. We pray as Jesus taught us, *"Your kingdom come, your will be done, on earth as it is in heaven"* (Matt. 6:10). Let Heaven come in your midst right now as you read this, in Jesus' Name.

Listen friend, God cannot become more near to you than living inside you! Psalm 34:18 talks about the Father being near to the brokenhearted and rescuing those who are crushed in spirit, this was a promise made *before* the cross. This was His promise for His people who were crushed. This promise is not only true today, but the nearness of God is even sweeter because as His children we have the Spirit of God living inside us! He mends us from the inside out! Wrap your heart around this truth today, friend! This is like honey. No longer is He the God afar, He is the God who is near. *He dwells within you*! Your heart has become His home.

> *Jesus replied, "Anyone who loves me will obey my teaching. My Father will love them, and we will come to them and make our home with them."* —John 14:23

THE CASE IS CLOSED—*NOT GUILTY!*

For centuries the "guilty" verdict hung over the head of humanity. And as though to dig the knife into our severed relationship with the Father even deeper, the devil, our accuser, was quick to remind us, *"you're guilty as charged...you'll never be good enough...you're guilty of betraying God, you're broken..."* and so on. But the blood of Jesus broke that curse and obliterated the power the enemy had on humanity. Now, having been bought with a price, we are free to live the abundant life of Christ as God's children!

Try as he might, the enemy can do *nothing* but lie to us now because the truth is that Jesus broke the curse when He died on the cross, the case is closed and we are deemed "not guilty" through Christ Jesus our Lord!

*Therefore there is now no condemnation [**no guilty verdict**, no punishment] for those who are in Christ Jesus [who believe in Him as personal Lord and Savior]. For the law of the Spirit of life [which is] in Christ Jesus [the law of our new being] has set you free from the law of sin and of death. For what the Law could not do [that is, overcome sin and remove its penalty, its power] being weakened by the flesh [man's nature without the Holy Spirit], God did: He sent His own Son in the likeness of sinful man as an offering for sin. And He condemned sin in the flesh [subdued it and overcame it in the person of His own Son], so that the [righteous and just] requirement of the Law might be fulfilled in us who do not live our lives in the ways of the flesh [guided by worldliness and our sinful nature], but [live our lives] in the ways of the Spirit [guided by His power]. For those who are living according to the flesh set their minds on the things of the flesh [which gratify the body], but those who are living according to the Spirit, [set their minds on] the things of the Spirit [His will and purpose]. —Romans 8:1-5 AMP*

This is good news, friend! God says over you, through the blood of His Son, "as far as the east is from the west I will remember your sins no more" (see Ps. 103:12)! The east to west is a perfect circle.

It never stops…it is eternal. So eternally speaking, you have been deemed *Not Guilty*!

BORN AGAIN?

*If you declare with your mouth, "Jesus is Lord," and believe in your heart that God raised him from the dead, you will be saved. For it is with your **heart** that you believe and are justified, and it is with your mouth that you profess your faith and are saved.* —Romans 10:9-10

Closing this chapter, I want to talk to those who aren't quite sure if they are "saved." Or, to those of you who would say you're not quite feeling assured in your salvation. Perhaps there's a looming question mark you can't seem to shake. You may feel too far gone or you may still be lingering on that *one* thing from your past. Friend, it's time for you to let that go! It's time to simply receive the gift of salvation by believing in the One who gave up His life and became sin on the cross bearing the full punishment for your sin in your place. He gave His life for you, now it's your turn to give your life to Him. He's waiting for you with arms open wide, a heart filled with love, in eager anticipation of your arrival. Simply pray this prayer with all your heart,

Dear Jesus, I ask you now to forgive me. I have sinned, I have hurt You, I have hurt others and I have hurt myself. Forgive me. Wash me. Cleanse me. Make me new. I ask you now to be my Savior, be my Lord and my very Best Friend. From this moment on I am Yours, and You are mine. From this moment on I give myself to You. In Jesus' Name, amen. (Prayer in Memory of Steve Hill, Evangelist 1954-2014.)

*We are therefore Christ's ambassadors, as though God were making his appeal through us. We implore you on Christ's behalf: **Be reconciled to God.*** —2 Corinthians 5:20

Perhaps you say, I'm a believer. I've been a believer my entire life. Or, I've been going after God with all my heart for months or even years now. Well, hooray! *Hallelujah!* Today, I pray you receive a fresh touch from Heaven! I pray God breathes on the embers of your heart! That your heart feels revived in God's presence as you are reading this now! Deep crying out to deep…spring up, oh well, within your soul! In Jesus' Name.

> *God has given us eternal life, and this life is in his Son. Whoever has the Son has life; whoever does not have the Son of God does not have life.* —1 John 5:11-12

What was once impossible, being near to God, is now made possible because of the cross and the blood of Jesus. And you were created to receive this gift from the Father and have no separation between you and Him. He desires you, friend. He loves you so much. *You are His beloved child!*

What is He saying to you?

_____

_____

_____

_____

_____

_____

_____

_____

_____

_____

_____

_____

_____

PART 2

Identity—Know Who You Are and Who God Is

Chapter 6

YOU ARE A CHILD OF GOD

*For those who are led by the Spirit of God are
the children of God. The Spirit you received
does not make you slaves, so that you live in fear
again; rather, the Spirit you received brought
about your adoption to sonship. And by him we
cry, "Abba, Father." The Spirit himself testifies
with our spirit that we are God's children.*
—ROMANS 8:14-16

I fell to my knees as the presence of God filled the room. It was a Thursday night and my six-year-old daughter and I had just left dance class, for her *not* me, in case anyone was wondering or concerned. *Ha!* I had been feeling a deep stirring to go to our local House of Prayer, PHOP, which was located only a couple blocks away from her dance studio. I said to my daughter, "Mommy would *really* love to go to PHOP and pray—would you like to come with me?" I watched as her little wheels turned, so to speak, and I could also tell Holy Spirit was stirring in her heart as her eyes met my gaze. Quietly I prayed for the desire of her heart to match the desire of mine and sure enough with a big smile she said joyfully, "Mommy, I would *love* to go pray with you."

I wish I could include the photo of her in her little purple and pink dance leotard kneeling in an empty room worshiping God as beautiful worship music flowed from the speakers overhead. We had arrived early so there was just a worship CD playing but the presence of God was already so heavy. We didn't waste any time. As I got my things settled, my little ballerina knelt down in front of me, extended both arms, closed her eyes, and worshiped Jesus. I settled in right behind her and did the same. As people began filing in, I could hear their faint gasps and whispers. *Ah, look how sweet...Oh, how precious...Thank you, Lord...*were among the most common comments as the people entering the room observed this precious little angel peacefully and reverently worshiping our Lord.

As the worship team set up and began to play, I was overwhelmed at the love of the Father. Now singing along to the music, I began thinking about how precious our relationship with the Father is. My daughter had now transitioned from worshiping to coloring and occasionally dancing and twirling. I love how unrestricted she is in the presence of God. She drew pictures of hearts and the cross and Jesus on the cross along with pictures of her mommy and daddy. *She is so free.* She knows who she is. She feels safe. Secure. Rooted in her identity as a daughter.

As the sounds of worship filled the room, my heart was filled with the warmth of God's love. Suddenly, I was overwhelmed by a vision the Lord began showing me as I knelt down, face in hands, and watched as it all unfolded in my spirit as a movie.

FROM ORPHAN TO DAUGHTER

Standing before a mirror I could see a young girl gazing at her reflection with tears in her eyes. She had just been adopted and had finally gotten a moment to herself away from her new *parents* to process the moments of the day. Staring at her reflection, she recalled the look of pure joy on the faces of her new *mom* and *dad* as they drove her home. As excited as she was to finally have a home and a family of her own, she still had a feeling something was missing. She had dreamed of this day her whole life. Here she was having just been given everything she ever hoped for and yet she experienced a lingering feeling within she couldn't quite put her finger on.

Staring at her reflection in the mirror, she wondered if she would somehow *look* different now that she was part of a family. Gazing into her own eyes and then examining her frame, she didn't *see* any noticeable difference. The person she saw standing before her was still an orphan, someone without a home—a *misfit* without a place to fit in.

She considered her new family and the love radiating from them. She didn't understand how they could love her so much, having only known her a short time. *"Where does their love come from,"* she asked herself. *"I don't understand,"* her heart cried.

Day after day she would stand before herself in the mirror and, looking deep into her eyes, she would remind herself of this simple truth: *I am no longer an orphan...I am someone's daughter now...I have a home...I have a place where I fit...Parents who love me and accept me for who I am....* But she struggled to really *see* herself any different. Day after day she was immersed in the intense love her parents had for her. Their love was consistent. It never faltered. It only grew deeper and deeper as the days rolled by. She found herself longing to accept their love but she was having a hard time as she scrutinized all the terrible things she had done in her past. All of the mistakes she had made. The rejection she still felt having been abandoned at such a young age. Yet the more her parents learned about her, her past, and her failings, the more they seemed to love her and accept her. *It was all so unreal.*

Finally, one day, as she studied herself in the mirror as she had every day since arriving *home,* something happened. She looked different somehow. Her perception of herself began to shift and on this particular day, locking eyes with herself in the mirror, she could see her parents—her mother and father—staring back at her with that fervent love she had come to know so well. She closed her eyes and when she opened them, tears flooded out as a river because the individual she saw staring back at her in the mirror was that of a *daughter*! Gone was her identity as an orphan. Leaning in a little closer, she stared deep into her eyes and there she saw it. Love. Love for herself and love for her parents. She saw love staring back at her and it was this love that defined who she was this day—a *daughter*. She no longer identified with being an orphan. She had found a home with her family who loved her, chose her, and accepted her, and as a result she was overcome with love for them—her *mother* and *father*! Their love redefined who she was and how she saw herself. She believed what they said about her—that she was loved and cherished! Her parents' love transformed her reality into what was truth, because she was indeed somebody's daughter. She hadn't been an orphan for quite some time now. And finally, for the first time, she could see it—*the Truth*.

Friend, this intense love is the love the Father has for you and then some! His love defines who you are—His beloved *child*. The moment you believed in Jesus—in His death, burial, and resurrection, that He is the Son of God who died for you, the prophesied Messiah, King of your heart—you are given the *right* to become His child (see John 1:12)! You have been given the Spirit of Sonship. The relationship that Jesus has with the Father, you now enjoy as a child of God! Today, allow that to shape how *you* see yourself. *You're a child of God.*

> *But to all who believed him and accepted him, he gave the right to become children of God. They are reborn—not with a physical birth resulting from human passion or plan, but a birth that comes from God.* —John 1:12-13 NLT

Perhaps for you, that moment of believing on Jesus was only moments ago in Chapter 5 as you read about the cross and the way that was made for you. Maybe you made a fresh commitment to surrender yourself to Him wholly, having read through part 1 of this book, believing that God cares deeply for you, and you are hearing His voice afresh and anew, surrendering all. Or maybe you're like me—you've been a believer most of your life yet the cross has become more and more real as you've grown in the Lord. Each of us has our own unique story to tell but we share this in common—as believers, we are children of the Living God and this reality should shift our perspective of ourselves, of God, and of others. Today, believe that God calls you daughter/son. Believe that you have a home in His heart and you are defined by who He says you are, not who you or anyone else says you are.

HE AFFIRMS YOUR WORTH

Then the woman, seeing that she could not go unnoticed, came trembling and fell at his feet. In the presence of all the people, she told why she had touched him and how she had been instantly healed. Then he said to her, "Daughter, your faith has healed you. Go in peace." —Luke 8:47-48

Looking back at the woman with the issue of blood from Luke chapter 8, I can hear the voice of the Father speaking through the Son as He affirms this precious woman's worth, *"Daughter,* your faith has healed you. Go in peace."

And that's what the Father says over you now: *Daughter...Son...* He's declaring His love for you affirming your worth, your value, and your identity as His beloved son or daughter.

Whatever it is that you need, see it in Jesus. Is it a healing? It's in Jesus. The woman in the story knew this. She had faith. It was her faith that drove her to her knees at the Savior's feet, and at His feet she discovered who she was, *a daughter.* Through the Son, the Father spoke words of value and worth not only confirming her healing, but also her identity as His daughter.

I remember one night when I was on my face before the Lord, I heard Him say to me, "Everything you need is at My feet. If you need *healing*, it's at My feet. *Freedom*, it's at My feet. *Joy...Peace...Forgiveness...*It's at My feet."

Friend, what is it that you need right now in this moment? What is stirring in your heart? Jesus has it for you. He is everything and He has everything for you. The Son entered into this world with a fierce focus, which was to find the lost sheep and return them to the Father. He restores sons and daughters to their Abba Father.

In Chapter 1, we discussed how much God cares for us. That He knows the number of hair on our heads. He even knows how many grains of sand are in the earth and how many stars hang in the sky, yet He knows you by name. But today I want you to grab hold of yet another powerful truth—not only does God know you by name, but also He created all of this just for you. He hung the stars in the sky so that you would have something to marvel at. What was once a blank canvas, God created and painted a landscape of love. With His voice He created the heavens and the earth. With four words light filled the darkness and then when the stage was set and the backdrop of creation was nearly complete, from the dust of the earth God created man, the crown of His creation, His masterpiece. He fashioned man in His own image and breathed life into his nostrils. It's truly marvelous and requires faith to believe.

> *By faith we understand that the u erse was formed at God's command, so that what is seen was not made out of what was visible.* —Hebrews 11:3

Open your heart and accept that God loves you. God has a plan for you. He wants to use you to further His Kingdom here on the earth, and He wants to empower you with His strength as you yield to Him so that you can do anything and everything He has marked for to do! Choose to believe what God says about you. Choose to believe that God is *for* you!

"Not by might nor by power but by my Spirit," says the Lord Almighty! —Zechariah 4:6

His Relentless Pursuit

God demonstrates His love by the lengths He was willing to go through to restore you to fellowship with Himself and to identity you as His child. Consider the parable of the lost son found in Luke 15.

Jesus continued: "There was a man who had two sons. The younger one said to his father, 'Father, give me my share of the estate.' So he divided his property between them.

"Not long after that, the younger son got together all he had, set off for a distant country and there squandered his wealth in wild living. After he had spent everything, there was a severe famine in that whole country, and he began to be in need. So he went and hired himself out to a citizen of that country, who sent him to his fields to feed pigs. He longed to fill his stomach with the pods that the pigs were eating, but no one gave him anything.

"When he came to his senses, he said, 'How many of my father's hired servants have food to spare, and here I am starving to death! I will set out and go back to my father and say to him: Father, I have sinned against heaven and against you. I am no longer worthy to be called your son; make me like one of your hired servants.' So he got up and went to his father.

"But while he was still a long way off, his father saw him and was filled with compassion for him; he ran to his son, threw his arms around him and kissed him.

"The son said to him, 'Father, I have sinned against heaven and against you. I am no longer worthy to be called your son.'

"But the father said to his servants, 'Quick! Bring the best robe and put it on him. Put a ring on his finger and sandals on his feet. Bring the fattened calf and kill it. Let's have a feast and celebrate. For this son of mine was dead and is alive again; he was lost and is found.' So they began to celebrate. —Luke 15:11-24

In this parable, we see the son demand his portion of the estate only to squander it all on "wild living." By his own omission, he finds himself living as an orphan, without a home, without an inheritance, scraping by in the pig trough, until one day he wakes up and realizes what he has done. He realizes in verse 17 how much better off he'd be in his father's home as a mere servant. I believe the son is having a revelation of his father's love. He's coming to realize it wasn't just money he inherited as his father's son; it was his father's heart. It was his love and his affection. Hoping for mercy, the son returns home willing to live as a mere servant in his father's house in order to return home and live under his father's loving care.

It's clear that son didn't fully understand the love, compassion, and mercy of his father. However, he was getting close. For him to acknowledge how well the *servants* were cared for in his father's house is an indication that his eyes were opening to the *nature* of his father. *"Wow, even the servants in my father's house are well cared for…"* Having left so quickly after receiving his financial inheritance, we can assume he lacked perspective on what it really meant to be a son, but suddenly the veil is beginning to lift as he decides to return home.

The son departing his old life and returning to his father is a beautiful picture of repentance. We leave our old life, not looking back, and turn our hearts to God, our Heavenly Father. And what do we find in verse 20? Do we see the son running to the father begging for forgiveness *before* the father embraces him? No, we see the father waiting in eager anticipation for the return of his lost son, and the moment the father sees the son *a long way off,* he runs to him! He embraces him and welcomes him home!

How powerful, friend! The moment the father spots the son, he runs to him! And then we see the son repenting to the father and the father responding by placing a robe on his back and a ring on his finger. He throws a party in the son's honor, celebrating his return home!

This is a beautiful picture of the heart of our Heavenly Father as conveyed by Jesus. Jesus shares this story with the Pharisees and teachers of the law in Luke 15 after being confronted about keeping company with "sinners." Jesus' fellowship with the lost, the "sinners," is a picture of the celebration feast thrown in honor of the lost son from the parable. Jesus doesn't ostracize the lost that are found in Him, He dines with them. He fellowships with them and teaches them. He *is* the very robe of righteousness draped around their shoulders and the ring of sonship they wear on their finger!

THE LOST SHEEP

Ripping open eternity, God placed His Son here on earth as the Good Shepherd going after the lost sheep, leaving behind the ninety-nine to find the *one*. By dining with "sinners," Jesus demonstrates that He really was the Shepherd who left all of eternity to enter the world filled with lost sheep.

By this time a lot of men and women of doubtful reputation were hanging around Jesus, listening intently. The Pharisees and religion scholars were not pleased, not at all pleased. They growled, "He takes in sinners and eats meals with them, treating them like old friends." Their grumbling triggered this story.

Suppose one of you had a hundred sheep and lost one. Wouldn't you leave the ninety-nine in the wilderness and go after the lost one until you found it? When found, you can be sure you would put it across your shoulders, rejoicing, and when you got home call in your friends and neighbors, saying, 'Celebrate with me! I've found my lost sheep!'

> *Count on it—there's more joy in heaven over one sinner's rescued life than over ninety-nine good people in no need of rescue.* —Luke 15:4-7 MSG

I can almost imagine a smile on His face as He shares this with them. Here He is. Jesus. Sitting with the very ones He came to save! He's sharing of the celebration happening in Heaven as they have found their home right here in Jesus, the Son of God! What joy it must have brought Jesus to scoop up the lost. What the Pharisee meant as a confrontation, Jesus shifted into a celebration! Though they may not have realized it at the time, we can see it as we read the testimony. *Jesus is celebrating!* He's conveying that He's the Shepherd who has found His lost sheep!

If you'll read further into Luke chapter 15, Jesus gives other examples of lost things being sought after and found,and the celebration that follows. Friend, it is critical you realize: you matter to God. You are everything to Him. You are His creation, formed in His own image and likeness. You represent a very special, unique attribute of the Father. God wants you to move past your limitations and hindering thoughts to believe what He says about you and believe today, once and for all, who *He* says you are. He thinks you can do anything! You are His child. He loves you. You don't need to clean up your act to be loved by God. God pursues you even before you've repented for straying. It's His kindness that leads us to repentance (see Rom. 2:4). Jesus chose fellowship with those who were known "sinners." In this He demonstrates a valuable lesson, that just as He came into the earth prior to, He draws near you prior to your repentance. It's His very presence that should lead you to repent and turn your heart to Him, leaving your old life and accepting His gift of the new life in Christ by the blood of Jesus.

> *Therefore, if anyone is in Christ, the new creation has come: The old has gone, the new is here!* —2 Corinthians 5:17

Slip into this reality. Let His robe of righteousness drape over your shoulders now as you breathe in the life-giving breath of God and breathe out the stress, weight, shame, and guilt you've been carrying. God has peace for you today, friend! He has a ring of sonship ready to slip on your finger, even now. Simply reach out your hand as the woman did with the issue of blood and see Jesus as His gaze fixes on you, affirming you as *"Son. Daughter."*

You Are The Beloved of God

One night I was dreaming. It was more of an abstract dream filled with vibrant colors, shapes, and sounds. What started out as simple and flowing began to crescendo into fast-moving frenzied swirls of vibrant color and fast music. The colors and sounds were thundering in my dream as though responding to the beat of a drum whose drummer had become a bit unhinged! It was loud and chaotic and I could feel my heart beginning to race until suddenly the alarm on my phone began to play. Slicing right through the hectic sounds of my dream were the sweet melodic chords of the song, "My Beloved" by Kari Jobe. I quickly turned my alarm off so as to not wake my husband, who was sound asleep next to me; it was 4:30 A.M. after all. As I lay my head back on my pillow staring up at the dark ceiling, I was relieved to have been awakened from that crazy dream. The beautiful melody from the song on my alarm filled my mind, *you're My beloved you're My bride, to sing over you is My delight...* and then I heard the Holy Spirit say, "That's what the Father does, He slices right through all the chaos with this beautiful message that you're His beloved."

Beautiful isn't it? Think about that for a moment. Think about the great lengths the Father went through to get His Son here. Ripping open eternity to place Him among humanity, bound by His love for us and limited *only* by His desire to yield to the Father's plan—not His own will but the Father's will be done.

This is powerful, friend! His desire for us, His love, His plan, and His purpose cut through all the chaos in our lives! All the lies! All the doubt, the fear, the worry, and sin—anything that may be thundering in our lives at the moment. Hearing from the Father's heart pierces through it all while planting a message of hope in our hearts. He plants His love song in our hearts and plays His melody of affection over us, restoring us to our position as His beloved through the blood of His Son. Wooing us to His chambers where He eagerly awaits our willingness to join Him.

> *The Lord your God in your midst, The Mighty One, will save; He will rejoice over you with gladness, He will quiet you with His love, He will rejoice over you with singing.*
> —Zephaniah 3:17 NKJV

It's the cry of His heart that we come away with Him, that we desire Him, and that we find rest and refuge in Him. Just as King David expressed in the Psalms, it's His promise for us that He will lead us beside still waters and quiet our soul (see Ps. 23:2–3).

He calls you His beloved. He calls you beautiful, *so* beautiful. He sings over you a song of peace. You have an opportunity to cast all your cares at His feet (see Ps. 55:22). Will you? When you do your burdens lift from your shoulders and you become *His*. He blankets you with His peace. He breathes His life inside of you. Where you once felt dry and weary He breathes new life into you. Dry bones come alive (see Ezek. 37)! He lifts you up on eagle's wings where you can soar peacefully above all that once weighed you down. You are given a fresh perspective.

YOU'RE HIS CHILD—HE'S PROUD OF YOU

I'm proud of you. This is something my dad would say to me often as I was growing up and still does to this day. This statement has shaped my life and my identity. He declared it enough that I never really felt the need to go out of my way to make him proud. As far back as I can remember, my dad would utter these very important words to me. But the thing that made the most impact on *who* I am is that he didn't just say this after some major achievement or accomplishment, he would say it in the quiet of the day for no apparent reason at all. Before closing my bedroom door at night, he would pop his head in one last time to sort of bookend my day with the words, "*I love you and I'm proud of you.*" As a result I knew at a young age that I made my dad proud simply because of who I was and not for what I did. It wasn't about what I could *bring to the table*. I am his daughter. There wasn't anything I could do or not do that would shift my father's perspective of me. I consider this one of my greatest gifts in life—having an amazing earthly father who beautifully demonstrates the nature of my Heavenly Father.

God wants *you* to know today, friend, that He's proud of you. When He looks at you, He sees His child. You don't have to jump through any hoops to make your Heavenly Father proud; He loves you, He sees you, and He accepts you for *you*. It breaks my heart when I hear people tremble over making their loved ones proud. They say of their parents or their spouse or even their own children, with anxiety in their eyes, "I just want to make them proud..." or "I sure hope I can make them proud." Yes, we make people proud through acts of service and achievement, sure, but it's when you know that God loves you for *you* that you'll begin to rest in who He says you are. You make God proud simply by believing what He says about you—*you're His child*, period. Believe it today, friend. Believe that He looks at you with Fatherly eyes of affection and love. He's proud of you whether you succeed or don't succeed. He's just plain proud of you because you're *His* and you declare Him *yours*.

I am my beloved's and my beloved is mine. —Song of Songs 6:3

EVERYDAY IMPACT

How does knowing who we are in Christ impact our everyday life and interactions with people? Because knowing who we are in Him and resting in that truth brings peace. And when we function from peace, we live peaceful lives. Sure storms will come but Jesus shows us what peace looks like during a storm—*trust*. During the storm, Jesus knew no harm would befall them as they sailed across the lake, so He slept (see Luke 8:23). When the disciples couldn't take it anymore and questioned why He was sleeping, He got up, rebuked the storm, and then admonished His disciples for their lack of faith. It's as though the disciples were supposed to follow His lead but they missed that mark. They didn't know that their eyes were to be fixed on Jesus and they were to do as Jesus did. Jesus was at peace and that should have been enough for them to trust that everything would be OK.

How you see yourself is the lens you view the world through. That is why it is critical we see ourselves the way God sees us.

This helps us in our everyday life because as God's children we have the same Spirit that raised Jesus from the dead living inside of us (see Rom. 8:11)! We can rely on our trust in the Lord and the peace that follows. Life brings storms. But we are to walk in peace and the assurance of who we, which is rooted in who He is. We aren't tossed about by the waves of culture or by what others think about us because we are rooted and anchored in who we are in Christ. Like Jesus, we are defined by what *God* says about us and not by what man says or thinks of us.

> *As soon as Jesus was baptized, he went up out of the water. At that moment heaven was opened, and he saw the Spirit of God descending like a dove and alighting on him. And a voice from heaven said,* **"This is My Son, whom I love; with him I am well pleased!"** —Matthew 3:16-17

This is what the Father does for His children—He declares from the heavens over you even now, *"You are my beloved child and I am proud of you."*

A once impossible reality for us to live in becomes possible by the blood of the Lamb! We realize we were created for purpose and on purpose. As God's beloved children, suddenly every promise of God becomes available to us through Christ. Please, allow your faith to be stirred for the impossible as you read on. God has more in store for you, friend. We're just getting started!

What is He saying to you?

Chapter 1

GOD'S PROMISES

Now if we are children, then we are heirs—
heirs of God and co-heirs with Christ, if
indeed we share in his sufferings in order
that we may also share in his glory.
—ROMANS 8:17

All of God's promises are "yes" in Christ and "amen" when our hearts come into agreement! We hold the keys to the Kingdom and as we read above; we are heirs of God *with* Christ! Scripture clearly states in Second Corinthians 1:20, *"For no matter how many promises God has made, they are 'Yes' in Christ. And so through him the 'Amen' is spoken by us to the glory of God."*

Our inheritance as His children is incredible! Yet sometimes we can't see what's right in front of us. Why? There are a number of reasons. Pride, envy, jealousy, doubt, and blindness all hinder us from being fully aware of what we possess as God's beloved kids. Paul pointed out that on earth we still see "dimly" the realities of Christ (see 1 Cor. 13:12). This is why the deeper the love relationship with Christ, the more clearly one will see the spiritual realities.

In the last chapter, we examined Jesus' parable about the prodigal son, viewing it from the perspective of the younger son who squandered his financial inheritance and then found his way home to the wide-open arms of his father. In this chapter, I'd like to pick up where we left off and observe the story from the older son's perspective, the son who had stayed with his father and was stunned when he discovered the celebration the father threw in honor of his brother.

> *Meanwhile, the older son was in the field. When he came near the house, he heard music and dancing. So he called one of the servants and asked him what was going on. "Your brother has come," he replied, "and your father has killed the fattened calf because he has him back safe and sound."*
>
> *The older brother became angry and refused to go in. So his father went out and pleaded with him. But he answered his father, "Look! All these years I've been slaving for you and never disobeyed your orders. Yet you never gave me even a young goat so I could celebrate with my friends. But when this son of yours who has squandered your property with prostitutes comes home, you kill the fattened calf for him!"*
>
> *"My son," the father said, "you are always with me, and everything I have is yours. But we had to celebrate and be glad, because this brother of yours was dead and is alive again; he was lost and is found."* —Luke 15:25-32

The older son's focus is on the wrongdoing of his brother. All he can see are his mistakes. How he squandered the father's financial inheritance. He's missing the point all together, that his younger brother was being welcomed back home as a *son*. His father is essentially demonstrating what sonship looks like! Let's take a look at verse 32 in the Amplified Bible,

But it was fitting to celebrate and rejoice, for this brother of yours was [as good as] dead and has begun to live. He was lost and has been found. —Luke 15:32 AMP

In essence, this is what occurs when the lost are found, there's a celebration! What a picture of mercy and grace! We don't get what we deserve, we get what Christ died for, restoration to the Father! There's no condemnation in Christ Jesus—there's *celebration*!

Similar to the older son in this story, it can be easy for us to overlook our spiritual inheritance—what we already possess as God's children. Often we get angry and/or jealous when we see God fulfilling promises for others, quietly taking inventory of our own life, wondering why these things aren't happening to us. Friend—don't be like the older brother in this story and miss what you already possess and can never lose as God's child! God already gave His all for you and to you. He opened up the very chambers of His heart and gave you what was inside—His Son, *Jesus*. I love what Romans says, *"He who did not spare his own Son, but gave him up for us all—how will he not also, along with him, graciously give us all things?"* (Rom. 8:32).

Often the sense of entitlement becomes a hindrance, blinding us to what was made available for us through the blood of Jesus. What a shame! But it is so common. I believe each of us can relate to feeling this way at some point in our life, and if we are honest with ourselves and with God, we can overcome this. I have had to deal with this in my own heart and have brought it to the foot of the cross in repentance. Please, allow your eyes and heart to be open right now.

Did this ring true to you? Have you been dealing with a sense of jealousy toward others? Have you taken for granted what God has already given you—and gives freely without condition—and is giving you in your own life? He's already given you His Son! Through the blood of Jesus, every blessing becomes available for the believer (see Eph. 1:3). Everything He has He freely gives. If this was for you, please, fall to your knees now and repent to the Father for this sense of lack you've allowed to fester. Thank Him for His love, His grace, His forgiveness, and for the blessings we have in Christ Jesus our Lord!

IT'S A SPIRITUAL EXCHANGE

Late one night as I slept, my spirit was roaring within me. I could hear an orchestra thundering in the well of my soul! The sound was so full! I was hearing every instrument imaginable, all playing in perfect unison. It was heavenly! As I rolled around in my bed, I began hearing the Holy Spirit speaking to me. Over and over this one sentence tossed about as a wave crashing on my heart, *"It's a spiritual exchange of everything the Father has He freely gives."*

Suddenly, I woke from my sleep and with a sense of urgency jumped from my bed thinking, *I have to remember this!* Fumbling around in the dark, I searched franticly for a pen. Strangely, I found one on my bathroom counter. I then grabbed a piece of paper from I don't know where and wrote the words down: *It's a spiritual exchange of everything the Father has He freely gives.*

The next morning when I woke, the events of the evening began flooding back into my mind. *What was it the Holy Spirit was saying to me over and over again??* It was all a blur, I couldn't remember. I sat in my bed, closed my eyes, and suddenly recalled my frantic search for a pen in the dark. I jumped up and there, sitting on my bathroom counter, written in *red* ink, was that incredible sentence from the Father's heart. Where and how I had found a red pen in the middle of the night, and how it ended up on my bathroom counter, I had no clue. But the message was clear to me—God writes His promises upon our hearts in the blood of His Son. Our fates are sealed—we are His kids and everything the Father has, He freely gives us.

> *Draw near to God and he will draw near to you.*
> —James 4:8 ESV

GOD KEEPS HIS WORD

So is my word that goes out from my mouth: It will not return to me empty, but will accomplish what I desire and achieve the purpose for which I sent it."
—Isaiah 55:11

God keeps His Word and He never speaks a frivolous or empty word. Every word from the mouth of God has a purpose and a destination. Right now, think about what you've heard God say to you. Be encouraged, God is not a man that He should lie (see Num. 23:19) and His Word will not return void! It will accomplish what it was sent out to accomplish!

When God speaks, He creates. His Words have life! They cut to the heart. His Word is like water on a dry ground causing new life to spring forth! His Word stirs something in you. His Word causes dead hearts to come alive! Even dry bones rise up and life begins to flow into them,

> *The Lord took hold of me, and I was carried away by the Spirit of the Lord to a valley filled with bones. He led me all around among the bones that covered the valley floor. They were scattered everywhere across the ground and were completely dried out. Then he asked me, "Son of man, can these bones become living people again?"*
>
> *"O Sovereign Lord," I replied, "you alone know the answer to that."*
>
> *Then he said to me, "Speak a prophetic message to these bones and say, 'Dry bones, listen to the word of the Lord! This is what the Sovereign Lord says: Look! I am going to put breath into you and make you live again! I will put flesh and muscles on you and cover you with skin. I will put breath into you, and you will come to life. Then you will know that I am the Lord.'"*

So I spoke this message, just as he told me. Suddenly as I spoke, there was a rattling noise all across the valley. The bones of each body came together and attached themselves as complete skeletons. Then as I watched, muscles and flesh formed over the bones. Then skin formed to cover their bodies, but they still had no breath in them.
—Ezekiel 37:1-8 NLT

These bones Ezekiel stood among were not just dead, they were *very* dead! There was absolutely no life left in them whatsoever. They were dried out! In verse 3, God asks Ezekiel a question so mind blowing that it begins to stir Ezekiel's faith for the impossible,

Son of man, can these bones become living people again?

I can only imagine how blown away Ezekiel was that God would ask *him* such a question! Ezekiel responds,

Only you know the answer to that God.

In verse 4, God had a promise for what was dead and He uses Ezekiel as His mouthpiece to declare and stir up life! God says to Ezekiel (and I'm paraphrasing),

Ezekiel, you are going to speak a prophetic word to these bones. You're going to speak My word to them and declare that I'm going to put breath into them and make them alive again. You're going to speak to that which is dead and see life spring forth!

By faith and in obedience, Ezekiel spoke out the word the Lord gave to him for these dry bones and as we read above, it was just as Ezekiel spoke the word the Lord said that he began to hear a *rattling sound* coming from this valley of dried-up bones! How phenomenal! Almighty God, Creator of the u erse puts His Word of life into the mouth of man. The same creative power that flows from the mouth of Creator God, *Elohim*, now flows from the lips of Ezekiel! The bones begin to shake as Ezekiel called them forth from their grave with life-giving words. What was once dead, now life springs forth from within. Suddenly new life, muscles and flesh, formed over the bones. What was once dead can no longer be seen, the old has passed, the new has come!

> Then he said to me, "Speak a prophetic message to the winds, son of man. Speak a prophetic message and say, 'This is what the Sovereign Lord says: Come, O breath, from the four winds! Breathe into these dead bodies so they may live again.'"
>
> So I spoke the message as he commanded me, and breath came into their bodies. They all came to life and stood up on their feet—a great army. —Ezekiel 37:9-10 NLT

Ezekiel speaks the word as the Lord gives it and the winds obey blowing breath into the newly revived bodies and suddenly there was a great army before him! Each did their part. God released the command. Ezekiel obeyed, and so does the wind.

> Then he said to me, "Son of man, these bones represent the people of Israel. They are saying, 'We have become old, dry bones—all hope is gone. Our nation is finished.' Therefore, prophesy to them and say, 'This is what the Sovereign Lord says: O my people, I will open your graves of exile and cause you to rise again. Then I will bring you back to the land of Israel. When this happens, O my people, you will know that I am the Lord. I will put my Spirit in you, and you will live again and return home to your own land. Then you will know that I, the Lord, have spoken, and I have done what I said. Yes, the Lord has spoken!'" —
> Ezekiel 37:11-14 NLT

His Word was His promise. This once-dead army of bones represented the spiritually dead people of Israel who assumed they were too old and dried up to make any difference for God. All hope was gone. God's Word brings life and hope. It is never empty or without purpose. He doesn't speak a word without knowing its purpose and final destination. He wanted light in the beginning so He spoke the word. In this case, He wanted to bring life to what was dead and instead of speaking the word Himself, He releases His life-giving word to Ezekiel. In faith, Ezekiel prophesies with power and authority over the dead things to come alive!

God used Ezekiel to do the impossible. He empowered him with His Word showing him just what was possible with God. *Anything and everything*! Even life forming into completely dead, dried-up bones! And that is precisely what God does today. He gives you His Word and He tells you to use it. Speak it out! Release His Word of truth to a dying, dried-up world in need of hope! And what's more, He's given you His Spirit! The same Spirit that rose Jesus from the dead lives in you! You have been given the power and authority to launch life!

Has something died in you? Are you in need of hope? Speak this word over yourself right now; speak to those dreams inside of you that have begun to whither and die, and command them to spring to life in the Name of Jesus!

> *And I will do whatever you ask in my name, so that the Father may be glorified in the Son. If you ask me for anything in my name, and I will do it.* —John 14:13-14

YOUR DREAMS ARE MEANT TO COME TRUE

> *Trust in the Lord with all your heart and lean not on your own understanding; in all your ways submit to him, and he will make your paths straight.* —Proverbs 3:5-6

Just as God doesn't speak an empty or frivolous word nor does He plant a promise or a dream in your heart without purpose. Something I have learned through over a decade of living a dry life lacking vision—lacking purpose—is this: dreams are like plants—they need water to grow and thrive. And watering dreams happens in the secret place. It's in that quiet time of fellowship with our Lord that He sprinkles His life-giving water on what He's planted in your heart. Often we stop praying into our dreams because we don't see the fulfillment quick enough. Soon after we find discouragement has crept its way in like a lion stalking its prey. And then, seizing the opportunity, the enemy pummels us with his lies and accusations *"See...you were never going to accomplish that. You're not qualified for that. I told you God didn't really have a plan for your life. You're too far gone now."* Next thing we know we are living life settling for any good thing we can get our hands on in order to feel some semblance of validation because we're convinced God can't use us anymore. Sound familiar?

God plants dreams in your heart like seeds and He saturates the soil of your heart with His life-giving water to bring nourishment and growth. Dreams are glimpses of His promise and destiny for your life. If you're not spending time in His presence, you're not going to see those dreams grow into what God planted them for. He is the Gardener. He plants with purpose and He waters during your abiding time with Him. In the same way, He prunes us and we bear much fruit in this abiding time, which we discuss more in later chapters.

Friend, it's vital that you never stop watering your dreams! Never stop bringing them before the Lord and sowing into them through prayer. When God gives you a dream or a vision for your life, it doesn't mean it's going to come into fullness immediately. God's timing is much different than ours. It took me over a decade to realize this. But God is faithful and His promises are yes, and amen.

Today, God wants to unlock those dreams inside of you! He's calling out to dry bones, *"Come alive!"* He's calling out to dried-up dreams, *"Come alive!"* Commit to God that you're going to spend time with Him praying into your destiny allowing Him to water what's been planted. He has a plan and a purpose for your life!

DISCOURAGEMENT

Here's what the enemy wants to do: he wants to bring discouragement into your heart because you're not seeing God fulfill what He's promised. He lies to you that it's never going to happen. Friend, God doesn't give you vision for your life to discourage you, rather He shows you glimpses at what's ahead as encouragement in order that you'll begin praying into your destiny. Sowing seeds of faith into the good soil of the promised land, God is beginning to reveal to you for your life! Don't be like the Israelites grumbling and complaining as you walk along the path toward God's promise. Rather, open your eyes to the miracles happening every day. Thank God for His daily provision, *daily bread*. Thank God for Jesus and His blood because without Jesus, your life would look a lot different. Don't be like the entitled son in the parable of the lost son who was jealous that a party was being thrown in his brother's honor, all the while missing the beauty before him and the unbroken relationship he enjoyed with his father all those years. Celebrate others! Celebrate the victories in people's lives! And celebrate what God is doing today in your life while clinging to what He's promised for your future!

> *"For I know the plans I have for you," says the Lord. "They are plans for good and not for disaster, to give you a future and a hope."* —Jeremiah 29:11

KEEP YOUR EYES ON JESUS

> *Keep your eyes on Jesus, who both began and finished this race we're in. Study how he did it. Because he never lost sight of where he was headed—that exhilarating finish in and with God—he could put up with anything along the way: Cross, shame, whatever. And now he's there, in the place of honor, right alongside God.* —Hebrews 12:2 MSG

I remember being taught in drivers training to "drive ahead" which means you're not looking at the ground directly in front of you where your car is currently driving. If you did this, you would miss what's up ahead, which could be dangerous! And you're certainly not to be driving with your eyes concentrating on the rearview mirror, observing where you came from and what is behind you! Rather you're to be focused ahead. Your eyes are fixed forward on where you are going. Likewise, God gives us a vision for our life as a beacon for what is to come.

Ultimately, we are to keep our eyes fixed on Jesus. He is the mark. In the storm He is the lighthouse showing us where dry ground is. He guides our steps. He takes us by the hand and leads us through our destiny. Often we wonder, *what is my destiny? What is God's plan for my life?* I would like to propose to you, friend, in answer to your question, that you are living it right now! You're doing it—God's plan, God's destiny for your life—you're there. *You've arrived!* It's your *story.* The life you're living at this very moment is the story you'll tell. Your testimony. Often it's challenging to see clearly when we're in the moment. We need perspective to see—that old expression that hindsight is 20/20 vision. But what if God wants to give you 20/20 vision right now in the present?

My husband always says "acceptance comes before understanding." I love this! Though it may be difficult to *understand* what God is doing, you can simply *accept* that He is in control and therefore, there is a reason and a purpose for everything you're going through right now. For the season you are in. Even if it feels like a dry season, be encouraged—God makes a way in the wasteland and streams in the desert (see Isa. 43:19)! *It's His promise!*

Take a moment right now and allow gratitude to envelop your heart. Begin to thank God for your story. Thank Him that by the blood of His Son your story and His-story have become one. Say to Him with all your heart, "Abba, I accept that you have a plan for my life and though I may not understand your ways I know that Your ways are higher than my ways and Your thoughts are higher than my thoughts. I trust you God and what you are doing in my life. You are the carpenter and I am the tool that you can use in whatever way you have planned in order to carry out *Your* will and purpose for this planet. I say, 'yes' to you God. Have Your way."

"For my thoughts are not your thoughts, neither are your ways my ways," declares the LORD. —Isaiah 55:8

THERE ARE NO BLUEPRINTS

Do you ever wonder why God doesn't just give you a blueprint for your life? I know I've questioned this many times. One reason He doesn't give us the blueprint is simple really, because our minds are so limited. We would end up reducing God's plan to that which we can do in our own strength. Honestly—and I know the women readers will especially relate to this—what would we do if we had a full roadmap/blueprint for our future? *We would plan.* We would get in there and begin trying to figure it all out. In an effort to be "proactive" and "efficient," we would put our stamp on it, begin booking flights, looking for homes, pricing things out, and so on. Where is the faith in that, friend? We would get in there with all our limited "know-how" and would ultimately reduce the things of God for our life to that which is possible for us.

God doesn't want His children to live the life of what is possible, rather He wants to do the impossible through you! If He gave a roadmap and a blueprint, we would end up restricting the impossible things of God to what is possible in our own strength. In reality, I believe we would take one look at the map and reach for our big red editing pen, crossing things out, moving things, and so on. I imagine the inner dialogue for our blueprint editing would go something like this,

Nope, that is impossible…God must not have meant to put that in there.

Oh, there's another one…walking on water? Really?! God must not have meant that I would literally walk on the water, that's impossible! So I'll just

buy a boat that way, I know I can get across that body of water there. I know God has a plan to get me to the other side so this is good...I can help God out on this one.

Ooops, there's a mountain in the way here...Obviously I can't move mountains so I'll have to get some new shoes, some camping gear and a Jeep. Then I can go around that mountain and take another route to the other side so I can end up where God is wanting me to go...

What is this?! Look at all these sick people! I'll have to stock up on medical supplies here to ensure I've got what they need to get better.

Write a book?! Well that's exciting! I'll need to be qualified for that so I'll have to get a college degree and take lots of writing classes so that I can create good content and know what I'm doing to accomplish that element of God's plan.

Wow, three children! Clearly I'll need to save up a lot of money to get the fertility treatments I'll need since I'm barren. How exciting. I'm so glad God showed me that so I can get prepared and not be caught off guard.

And the list really could go on and on.

This is what Abraham did isn't it. God told Him in his old age that he and his wife Sarah, who was barren, would have a baby. Abraham figured he would help God out by getting another woman pregnant who could carry out the promise because it was "impossible" for his wife Sarah to have children (see Gen. 18:10). But with God, nothing is impossible and Sarah ended up having a baby just as the Lord had promised

> *The Lord kept his word and did for Sarah exactly what he had promised. She became pregnant, and she gave birth to a son for Abraham in his old age. This happened at just the time God had said it would. And Abraham named their son Isaac.* —Genesis 21:1-3 NLT

And what about Moses? What do you think He would have done if he had seen that he was going to lead the Israelites out of captivity by crossing *through* the Red Sea (see Ex. 14)? He would probably have brought a boat! They would likely have been so consumed pulling all the boats they would need that their timing would have been off, which could have resulted in them being taken captive again by the Egyptians, who were right on their tail as they fled Egypt.

My friend, don't reduce God's plan for your life to what you would consider "possible"! God gets glory when you allow Him to do the impossible through you! This is what He created you for! This is part of His plan and promise for your life! You were created for the impossible! Like Abraham, Moses, and David! Listen, sometimes the giant we need to slay or the sea we need to part is in our own limited thinking! Our limited thoughts and ideas can hinder our faith for the impossible things of God. Well, enough is enough! Won't you join me in breaking through the thoughts that hinder us from walking on water? From commanding that mountain in our way to *move!*

I don't have an English degree, I haven't taken any special writing classes and I don't have a massive audience, but what I do have is a promise! I have stewarded that promise—that *dream*—in prayer faithfully through the last 17 years of my life. Yes, there was a season where I put the dream on a shelf and nearly allowed it to die, but God is faithful! When God began to say to me four years ago, "*take a step...do something...sit down and start writing...*" I listened. Writing a book was part of God's plan for my life! And isn't it cool that He's using what I would consider *limitations* to give Himself the glory He deserves! He has paved the way for me with this book. And now as I write it, I'm blown away at the goodness of God and how He's using my story to convey *His*-story.

Sometimes the most impossible thing is to simply believe what God says about you.

CHOOSE TO BELIEVE GOD'S PROMISES

I choose to believe God when He says, *"Krissy, I think you can do anything!"* And now it's your turn, friend. Will you choose to believe what God says about you? Will you respond to His prompting and His leading for your life? Will you trust the Lord with all your heart, mind, soul, and strength, and lean not on your own understanding? *God thinks **you** can do anything!*

Something my dad always says to me is not to worry about outcomes, just do what's right. Often we think and think about the outcome and in doing so we allow fear to grip us and hinder us from taking that one simple step of faith Jesus asks us to take out of the boat atop the waters with Him. We are thinking, "I can't walk on water...I can't overcome this fear of storms, *look* at the wind! It's creating gigantic! There's no way I'll get to Jesus." When all the while Jesus is looking at you with eyes piercing right through the circumstances in your life, asking you to trust Him with one simple step. *That's it*—just one obedient step in faith. Will you take it? Will you step outside the boat today allowing those boundaries and ropes you've set up around yourself called "what's possible" to dissolve around you today? Step into the impossible with Jesus, friend...He's got you —it's His promise..

What is He saying to you?

_____

_____

_____

_____

_____

_____

_____

_____

Chapter 8

CREATED TO SHINE

You are the light of the world—like a city on a hilltop that cannot be hidden. No one lights a lamp and then puts it under a basket. Instead, a lamp is placed on a stand, where it gives light to everyone in the house. In the same way, let your good deeds shine out for all to see, so that everyone will praise your heavenly Father.
—MATTHEW 5:14-16 NLT

Sitting alone in an empty house, a feeling of deep despair bubbled up in my spirit as I cried out to God. My children were at school and my husband was at work. I treasure my mornings alone with God. On this particular morning, a battle was raging in my mind. My soul was in mourning as I began to wonder why certain aspects of my life hadn't played out the way I thought they would.

As I prayed I began to cry out, "Why God...Why is this so hard...I can't understand why these things aren't working out like I sensed they would...The way YOU showed me they were going to?!"

Tears flowed from my eyes as a raging river crashing through a newly broken dam. God spoke. *"Krissy..."* His voice was calm and Fatherly. *"You've been trying so hard to color inside the lines."*

Peace came over me instantly as I sat in His presence hanging on His every word. *"It's OK to color outside the lines,"* He continued. *"It's OK."* His Words echoed in my spirit. And that was all He said. But I got it.

There I sat eyes closed basking in the warmth of His presence. I began to imagine my kids as they colored. At the time, my daughter was in kindergarten and was very serious about staying inside the lines. In kindergarten there is such emphasis about developing this as a skill and she was always so proud of herself when she did, rightfully so. My son, however, who had just turned four was more of a free spirit by nature, and hadn't yet had that particular teaching in school. So when he colored it was all over the place! Though completely different approaches, each of my children colored from a place of joy and freedom.

Then, I began to reflect upon the scenario a little more and consider what happened when my daughter would challenge her brother's coloring.

"Buddy..." She would say with deep concern and a splash of irritation, "You're not doing it right. You're not coloring inside the lines. You're just scribbling!"

Most times my carefree son would just look at her, laugh, and then scribble bigger and more ostentatious than ever, but every now and then her words would hurt him. Every now and then her expectation would box him in and cause discouragement to drape over him like a heavy cloak, one that he lacked the strength and maturity to simply brush off. In these cases, big crocodile tears would begin to form in his sparkly blue eyes as he compared his paper with his sister's, noticing the vast difference between the two.

God used this to teach me a very powerful lesson about myself. That the once *out-of-the-box* aspects of myself had somehow gotten boxed *in*—I had gotten so concerned about fitting in when God made me to stand out. I was *afraid*—afraid of stepping out fully into the plan of God for my life. Afraid of running full speed ahead the path marked out for me. I had begun slowing down, nearly tip-toeing through life scared to death of messing up, saying the wrong thing, offending someone, failing, etc. Even the thought of succeeding scared me!

So here I sat—faced with a decision. Do I continue down the path of a careful existence, mindful of not stepping on any toes along the way? Or do I jump feet first into the life of freedom and purpose God had called me to—unafraid of coloring outside the lines? Embracing that I was created for the impossible! Created to shine! Created to reflect Jesus to a lost and broken world.

The words of Jesus echoed in my spirit once again as I felt my soul rising up in boldness, *"Never the less, not my will but your will be done Father."*

What discouragement had tried to cover, I will stand boldly and allow to shine—*Your will be done God*!

I wonder, how many of you can relate to this? How many of you are feeling that same stirring, that God wants you to let go of fear, embrace His call on your life, and color outside the lines? He has called you to stand out—not be *boxed in*. It's the life outside the boat. The life of the impossible. The life of running and dancing upon the waters of destiny with Jesus!

> *Arise, shine for your light has come and the glory of the Lord rests upon you.* —Isaiah 60:1

If this was for you, friend, why don't you take a moment with the Lord. Ask God to remove the cloak of discouragement so that His cloak of righteousness is all that remains! Rebuke the fear that has crippled you and declare freedom over yourself right now! Remember, the same Spirit that raised Christ from the dead lives in you (see Rom. 8:11)! So as a child of God you walk in authority and victory! You hold the keys to unlock your heart and set your feet to dancing! God is releasing JOY over you as you read this. Embrace that He has called you to stand out and not be boxed in.

LIGHT IN THE DARKNESS

John 1:5 says, *"The light shines in the darkness, but the darkness has not understood it."* That word *understood* in the Greek is, *katalambano,* which has a double meaning. It means to obtain, attain, take hold of; seize, overtake, grasp, understand, realize, and find out.

The darkness can neither overtake the light of Jesus nor can it understand it! And that is the light that shines through us! I love how the Amplified Bible relays this passage from John,

> *In the beginning [before all time] was the Word (Christ), and the Word was with God, and the Word was God Himself. He was [continually existing] in the beginning [co-eternally] with God. All things were made and came into existence through Him; and without Him not even one thing was made that has come into being. In Him was life [and the power to bestow life], and the life was the Light of men. The Light shines on in the darkness, and the darkness did not understand it or overpower it or appropriate it or absorb it [and is unreceptive to it].* —John 1:1-5 AMP

In the beginning *"the earth was formless and empty, darkness was over the surface of the deep, and the Spirit of God was hovering over the waters"* (Gen. 1:2). Then suddenly, the Father spoke *"Let there be light,"* (Gen. 1:3) and Light came forth from the mouth of God. Light was released and the darkness could neither stop it nor understand it! What a phenomenal moment to mark the beginning of time, friend! The spoken Word of God released from the Father's heart in that moment forever

SHINING BRIGHT: LIVING LIFE BY THE SPIRIT

But whenever someone turns to the Lord, the veil is taken away. For the Lord is the Spirit, and wherever the Spirit of the Lord is, there is freedom. So all of us who have had that veil removed can see and reflect the glory of the Lord. And the Lord—who is the Spirit—makes us more and more like him as we are changed into his glorious image.
—2 Corinthians 3:16-18 NLT

There's fluidity to life in the Spirit. Life without the Spirit is choppy. It's *works* based. It's effort by effort. It is much like living paycheck to paycheck. It's living work to work. Life in the Spirit ties it all together. The Holy Spirit serves as a connector of life's moments causing them to flow together. Through Him we are able to honor God in everything we do. As I'm doing the dishes, I'm spending time with the Lord, worshiping, praying, talking to Him, and listening. I have fellowship with Him in all things. Essentially, He's in everything I invite Him to be a part of. Like a best friend who enjoys spending time with you no matter what you are doing, so the Holy Spirit is our *Friend* and enjoys our fellowship anytime, anywhere!

Moving from glory to glory is a picture of the Holy Spirit being that common thread between encounters with God. We encounter His glorious presence and we begin to reflect the brightness of His glory upon ourselves as a mirror (see 2 Cor. 3:18). The Holy Spirit keeps us shining bright and the more we encounter God, the more we progress from glory to glory. This has been my life story! Encounter after amazing encounter with the Father, He has revived my heart, refreshed my soul, and shines bright upon me from the inside out. My intense love for Him shines through the darkness around me! Piercing the darkness with His marvelous light! Everywhere I go! In every circumstance!

I think this is why I love going into the dark places because I have grown so confident in His light shining through me. It brings about fearlessness from within that Christ is radiating out of me. I confuse, confound, and apprehend the darkness all around! I once hugged the demons right out of someone! This precious woman was being tormented. She had been dabbling with witchcraft and all kinds of junk. God sent me to hug her. When finished, she looked deep in my eyes and just said, "Thank you." She then hugged me for hugging her! Afterward she couldn't even stand. She just sunk deep into her chair and rested her head against the wall. She looked like a little girl who had just encountered a celebrity or something. Totally startstruck. But she was *Son*-struck. She had encountered the love of Jesus for her through me. He had a mission to win her heart. Remember, Jesus came to bind up the brokenhearted and set the captives free. And that night, He used me as His hands and feet to do just that for this precious woman! I carried His light into her world and the darkness couldn't stand it! It fled with one hug! Hooray for God!

WHY YOU MATTER

Sitting before a blank word document, I worshiped God as songs of praise filled the room from my little Bluetooth speaker sitting atop my dresser. Overwhelmed by the love of the Father, I began asking Him to show me His heart. I began imagining the union between the Father and the Son before the creation of the world. The words of Jesus rolled through my spirit, *"Father, bring me into the glory we shared before the world began"* (John 17:5 NLT). And then His prayer for all believers:

> *My prayer is not for them alone. I pray also for those who will believe in me through their message, that all of them may be one, Father, just as you are in me and I am in you. May they also be in us so that the world may believe that you have sent me. I have given them the glory that you gave me, that they may be one as we are one—I in them and you in me—so that they may be brought to complete unity.*

*Then the world will know that you sent me and have loved them even as you have loved me." —*John 17:20-23

Meditating on all of this, I began imagining the folds of a heart and how it seems to wrap around itself, protecting what's inside.

Is this what the Father's heart looks like? I wondered.

Is the Son What, or Who, is wrapped up so tightly within the folds of the heart of the Father?

Oh how I longed to be inside His heart to hear what He hears and see what He sees, even if just for a moment. I began to cry out to the Father a seemingly impossible prayer, but I eagerly desired to give it a shot. "Abba, if even just for a moment would you bring me into your heart so that I can see how you see?"

I could feel Him near. There was something about His presence that caused me to stand and move toward my closet where I could be in total seclusion with Him. Before I could get there, I stopped and turned toward my window. I sat on the edge of my bed looking out my window and waited. On what, I didn't know. I just knew this was a heavy moment with the Lord. Suddenly, I saw a little blonde head bopping around my back porch. I watched as my son wandered around the patio picking up toys, examining them, and looking closely at his sister's pink bug carrier as though something interesting was inside (*it was empty*). A question began bubbling in my spirit, "Is *this* what's in your heart God?"

I observed how my son was oblivious to the fact that I was watching him. Yet he felt safe and secure alone on the back porch. I thought about how being outside alone can foster independence in my children, yet my husband and I know they are absolutely safe as our yard is fenced in and we check on them more than they even realize. But to them, they are alone and independent. Away from mommy and daddy. At four and six years old, being outside *alone* is a big deal. What they don't realize is they are never actually alone. They are within an earshot of their mommy and daddy who are on the other side of the patio door tuned in to their children's voices. If they need us, we would hear them. If they cried out in pain, we would be right there.

Eventually, my son wandered back inside the house and I sat on my bed wondering if that was the answer to my heart's cry.

Suddenly, the lyrics of the worship song blaring from my little speaker hit my heart—*all I have is drawn to more of you*—and I was drawn into my closet, diving deeper into His heart. There I fell to my knees and cried out with hunger, "Bring me into your heart God…allow me to see how you see. If even just for a moment." I felt His presence saturate the small space where I knelt. I could feel His love so deeply. The lyrics of the song echoed my heart's cry, *"There's a stirring in my soul…deep is calling to deep again…all I am cries out for more of you!"*

Then, all of a sudden my mind was consumed with only one thought: brownies. Yes, *brownies*…You see, I had promised my son a few days prior that we would make brownies. The first day, we forgot. The second day, we ran out of time. Now today, we had decided we would make them before going to my grandparents' house for the day and that time was coming near. Here I was, immersed in this precious time to worship and write, asking Abba to bring me inside of His heart…to bring me *deeper* and all I could see was my son and the desires of his tender little heart. I imagined the look on his face if we *ran out of time* or *forgot* to make the brownies again today. With a surge of love, I pulled myself up from my knees and went into the kitchen with my children to make the brownies.

To my surprise, this was the smoothest baking experience I've had with my kids. We mixed, stirred, poured, and stuck them in the oven. They then went their separate ways and I returned to my little prayer oasis in my closet. As I closed the doors behind me, I reflected on the peaceful time we had just had in the kitchen. I really didn't feel as though I had even left the presence of God. I could feel the Lord with me through each sprinkle of flour and crack of the egg. He was there in my children's smiles and giggles. Then it hit me—I had been asking Him to show me His heart and all along He was unveiling it to me through my kids. Just as my children are at the center of my heart, so His children are at the center of His. The cry of Jesus' heart in John 17 is that we, you and me, could be one with Him as He and the Father are one. When God looks at you, He sees His Son shining through! That's why God cares about even the smallest details of our lives, friend, everyday things (like brownies). What's inside the Father's heart is His beloved…and that's you and me friend.

To some, this may sound too simple, but to many, I know you'll hear this and I pray the Holy Spirit stirs within you this beautiful truth: if you want to know what is inside of the Father's heart, just go take a look in the mirror, friend, because it's *you*. You are what He sees. You are what all of this is about. The things that move your heart, move his heart. You are His treasure!

I AM UNDONE

When Isaiah had the encounter in the throne room of God, he was overwhelmed at what he saw! The train of God's robe filled the temple. The angels and seraphim were flying around crying out to one another *"Holy, holy, holy is the Lord God Almighty! The whole earth is filled with His glory"* (Isa. 6:3). The whole *earth*. What a powerful thought that the angels in His presence are overwhelmed at the beauty and majesty of Almighty God and at the same time they are overwhelmed that the whole earth, the totality of His creation, is *filled* with His glory! It's as though they are admiring His awesome plan for humanity, that His creation flowed from the beauty of God and they can see what an awesome reflection of His glory it is!

Think about this. What were the angels seeing? What were they overcome with? David said, "All of creation declares your glory" (see Ps. 19:1).

Take a moment and look outside, friend. What do you see? The whole earth is a beautiful revelation of the glory of God! Now go look in the mirror, what do you see? *You* are a reflection of God's glory created in His image and likeness.

God creates beautiful things. You are His treasure, the crown of His creation! You are a product of the Father's love and His plan. You are a manifestation of His glory! God thought of you and then He created you. You've always been a part of the Father's plan. Have you ever thought about that? He doesn't make mistakes and He doesn't create anything, or anyone, without purpose. You are a piece of this eternal puzzle called *life*. The very breath of God breathed life into man in the very beginning. And now here you are, having been formed and fashioned in your mother's womb by the hands of your Creator, God. Jehovah. Yahweh. You are His masterpiece, and now by the blood of Jesus, you can rise up and shine the light of Christ and the glory of God to a world desperate for hope!

> *But we all, with unveiled face, beholding as in a mirror the glory of the Lord, are being transformed into the same image from glory to glory, just as from the Lord, the Spirit.*
> —2 Corinthians 3:18 NASB

THERE IS HOPE

Do you ever watch the news and wonder: *is there hope?* I can relate. The news can be very depressing if we allow it to be. But there is indeed hope, friend! And that hope lives and breathes inside of you!

Christ in you, the hope of glory. —Colossians 1:27

Reflect back on the passage from Isaiah 6. The angels and seraphim declaring, *"Holy, holy, holy is the Lord God Almighty! The whole earth is filled with His glory."* They are viewing the world, the earth from an eternal vantage point and what they see is the glory of the Lord filling the earth! And we've just read that Jesus' prayer to the Father was that we be filled with the same glory He, Jesus, experienced here on the earth (see John 17:5). And Colossians 1:27 declares that this mysterious glory is embedded within God's people! Could it be that what the angels are viewing in the earth is the glory of Christ saturating the earth through God's children? All those who are filled with His Spirit. All those who have said, like Paul, I've been crucified with Christ, it's no longer I who live but Christ living in me (see Gal. 2:20)! It's a phenomenal thing, friend.

> *For God, who said, "Let there be light in the darkness," has made this light shine in our hearts so we could know the glory of God that is seen in the face of Jesus Christ. We now have this light shining in our hearts, but we ourselves are like fragile clay jars containing this great treasure. This makes it clear that our great power is from God, not from ourselves.* —2 Corinthians 4:6-7 NLT

You were made to shine. You were created for the impossible! Christ living in you is hope of His glory for the world! But this is no accident and it's not an all-exclusive club that only some have access to—it's for *all* who believe! It was Jesus' prayer for *all* who would believe in the message of the Gospel that He and the Father would come and make their home inside of you, shining through you! Don't hide your light under a bushel any longer, friend. Rise up and be as a mirror reflecting the radiant light of Christ to the world all around you!

What is He saying to you?

_____

_____

_____

_____

_____

_____

_____

PART 3

Going Deeper

Chapter 9

THE SECRET PLACE: INTIMACY WITH GOD

Here's what I want you to do: Find a quiet,
secluded place so you won't be tempted to role-play
before God. Just be there as simply and honestly
as you can manage. The focus will shift from you
to God, and you will begin to sense his grace.
—Matthew 6:6 MSG

The secret place—that sweet place of solitude between you and God. The place where you're not tempted to "role-play" before God as our Scripture says. It's just you and Him. There's no hype. No noise. No performance. Just *presence. His* presence and *your presence. His* heart and *your* heart.

Jesus died for us to have access to our very own secret place encounters with the Father. That now, by His blood all can come near (see Eph. 2:13). And it's in this nearness where we find God— the *fullness* of God. We discover the wealth of His presence and the vast ocean of His love. It's in the deep with Him when we discover who He is, who we are, and why we were created. Our faith is stirred, our love enriched, and our heart grows more courageous!

There are many facets to God. As a diamond held up to the light reveals a multitude of cuts and angles, we notice the many dimensions of His character when spending time with God. The qualities of God are eternal. They are never-ending! When we think we've discovered all there is to find, we realize we've only just scratched the surface. Friend, diving deep into the heart of God is an unending excursion of His love! You'll never get bored or tired. It's an endless pursuit! There's always more of Him! God is limitless! His love is extravagant!

> *Oh, how great are God's riches and wisdom and knowledge! How impossible it is for us to understand his decisions and his ways! For who can know the Lord's thoughts? Who knows enough to give him advice? And who has given him so much that he needs to pay it back? For everything comes from him and exists by his power and is intended for his glory. All glory to him forever! Amen.* —Romans 11:33-36 NLT

Though impossible to ever fully know the thoughts of God, it's reassuring to grasp that He created us to search them out! We were created to dive deep into His heart and excavate the minerals and nutrients that lie in wait for us to discover. There is life to be found there. Precious gems of wisdom and truth! Though they may not appear to be much at first glance, it's upon picking them up that we discern their true value. Precious gems "in the rough" are rugged, appearing ordinary at first glance. It's only when they are polished and the edges are smoothed that their true beauty and value is revealed. God desires us to hold fast to the truths found in His presence as precious gemstones. It's through prayer, fasting, and good stewardship we discover how priceless and lovely these truths actually are. God is waiting for us to search out His heart, uncovering what's inside. The floor of His heart goes deeper and deeper the more time we spend there. He always has, and is, more than enough.

Your Heart, His Home

*Do you not know that **you** are God's temple and that God's Spirit dwells in you?* —1 Corinthians 3:16 ESV

What does the secret place look like? Well…to God it looks like *your* heart. For you it should look like *His* heart. It's the place of intimate encounter with Him. The place you go anytime, anywhere, any day that you just *need* Him. Jesus was often found praying. He snuck away often to go up to the mountain or the garden to pray. The Father's heart is where He found refuge and strength. For Jesus, it's all He knew. If Jesus needed time with the Father, how much more do we?

David had deep intimate encounters with God when he was in the caves. This was his sanctuary. That is where he found refuge. He was tucked away and hidden from everyone and everything, especially hidden from those pursuing to harm him. It wasn't that these caves were anything remarkable—God was there with David because David was there! David was a man after God's heart so when David sought the Lord, he found the Lord.

But as for me, I will sing of Your mighty strength and power; Yes, I will sing joyfully of Your lovingkindness in the morning; For You have been my stronghold And a refuge in the day of my distress. To You, O [God] my strength, I will sing praises; For God is my stronghold [my refuge, my protector, my high tower], the God who shows me [steadfast] lovingkindness. —Psalm 59:16-17 AMP

Your perspective of God impacts your secret place experience. Is He your refuge? Is He your strength? Are you running to Him with your problems? Are you placing life's challenging circumstances at

His feet? Do you trust Him with everything? Do you see Jesus as *everything*? God is the Alpha and Omega. He is Jehovah Jirah. He is El Shaddai. He is in everything and all things are held together by Him.

> *The Son is the image of the invisible God, the firstborn over all creation. For in him all things were created: things in heaven and on earth, visible and invisible, whether thrones or powers or rulers or authorities; all things have been created through him and for him. He is before all things, and in him all things hold together. And he is the head of the body, the church; he is the beginning and the firstborn from among the dead, so that in everything he might have the supremacy. For God was pleased to have all his fullness dwell in him, and through him to reconcile to himself all things, whether things on earth or things in heaven, by making peace through his blood, shed on the cross.* —Colossians 1:15-20

This should influence our perspective of God. From here we come before Him with our day. We come before Him with our children, our spouse, our friends, and our *issues*. We bring everything to Him and lay it all at His feet so that we are left with just us. We then give Him our heart, our mind, our will, our emotions, our tears, our fears, our joy, and our mourning. We lie before Him stripped down to the very core of ourselves and simply say, *"Here I am Lord! I am yours. And you are mine."* We do this daily. Some days we may find ourselves living in the secret place. It's here we encounter the mercy seat. It's here we find rest for our souls. And it's here we give ourselves to Him fully.

In the secret place all God is looking for is you. He's not looking for hype. He's not interested in performance. He doesn't care about what you're wearing or what you look like. He just wants *you*. He says, come as you are. Come to me.

I Am Here...

Let's revisit one of the stories from the Bible we've gone over a couple of times already. This time we're going to consider it with the secret place in mind.

> *The Master said, "Martha, dear Martha, you're fussing far too much and getting yourself worked up over nothing. One thing only is essential, and Mary has chosen it— it's the main course, and won't be taken from her."*
> —Luke 10:41-42 MSG

Reading this passage, I can't help but hear this fundamental message coming from Jesus, *I Am here.* In my spirit I perceive Him subtly, yet boldly affirming, "Mary has *chosen* better because *I Am* here. She is drawn to Me. Nothing else *really* matters." This important declaration of hope He speaks over us still today, *"I Am here."*

He walked in this promise. He embodied it. He brought this same sense of refuge with Him everywhere He went and though many were confounded by Him, others were drawn to Him, finding rest, hope, peace, and refreshing. Everything they needed they found in Jesus.

I Am here.

Remember the well encounter with the Samaritan woman in John 4? Jesus went to the well and after sitting down for a drink declared to the woman that *He* was *living water* for her. There was the time being tempted in the desert when He boldly proclaimed, "Man does not live on bread alone, but on every word of the Father" (see Matt. 4:4). Jesus was satisfied on the bread of His Father—His Word, His promise. It causes one to wonder: did He even enter the home of Martha and Mary to eat a meal? Or was it for this precious fellowship time with all who would draw near Him as Mary was doing.

Jesus was ushering in a new way for us, a New Covenant. One of life in the Spirit and resting in His presence versus a life of striving for perfection. Mary seemed to understand that. Something about her was drawn to that very place of rest in Jesus. Instead of a Promised *Land*, Jesus was the Promised *One*, the Messiah whom she had been waiting in eager anticipation for.

A LOVESICK BRIDE

His Spirit stirs lovesickness within our hearts. We ache for time in His presence. We yearn for moments of intimacy where we lay our head against His chest feeling His heartbeat. This is all done in the secret place, in the quiet. Where you realize God isn't looking at what you *do for Him*—He's looking at what you *bring to Him*. And what He wants you to bring is yourself—*your heart*. The secret place is our place of encounter. It is our time in the river where our hearts are smoothed out and purified, as the stones were smoothed out for David to pick up from the stream and sling at the giant. With purified hearts, God can use us as His instruments slaying every giant before us through the power and might of the Holy Spirit!

> *You will seek Me and you will find Me when you seek Me with all your heart.* —Jeremiah 29:13

Many feel a distance from God. They don't understand the intimacy available with Him. It's important that we earnestly seek Him. That we draw near with sincere hearts. There's this unbelievable desire that comes over us. As a bride to her bridegroom, there's a longing inside of us for Him. *An ache.*

Many can relate to an unexplainable throb deep inside. What you may not realize is that your soul is crying out for nearness to God. Your soul is *dry...thirsty*. I've seen it so many times before, there seems to be this deep wound inside of people's hearts that they can't quite put their finger on. They embark on an unrelenting search for answers when all they really *need* is Jesus. They need Holy Spirit. They need to take that inevitable step off the edge of the cliff and take the plunge into the waters of God's amazing love! Diving deep into His heart with abandon where healing exists and peace resides. Suddenly, everything that was weighing them down is what they leave behind, as they leap over the edge into God's ocean of unrelenting love!

GOD WANTS YOUR HEART, NOT YOUR OBLIGATION

God is not interested in lip service. God hears our heart. Many times Jesus would address people based on what He heard them *thinking*. He is looking at the motives of our heart. What are you bringing before Him? Is it your heart? Your life? *Your all*? Or are you simply praying so that you can say you prayed today? As though it's an item on your *to-do* list. God doesn't care about your to-do list, friend! He cares about your heart! He desires fellowship with you. As we discussed in Chapter 1, He wants to *know* (*ginōskō*) you! As Jesus addressed Martha, *"Martha, Martha you are worried and upset about many things but only one thing is necessary and Mary has chosen it!"* Mary chose intimacy. God would say the same to you today. He's asking you, which will you *choose*—intimacy, or duty? I can tell you from personal experience—God doesn't want your obligation He wants your heart.

My time in the secret place looks different every single day. Some days I'm in my closet. Some days I'm worshiping around my house. Other days it's through deep time in the Word where truth after truth is unveiled. I have days of weeping, days of dancing, and days of silence. There are even days when my secret place encounters are while I'm doing the dishes, taking a shower, folding laundry, or driving my car. I simply *enjoy* spending time with God so much I invite Him into every facet of my day.

Consider this: What if Martha had invited Jesus into the kitchen with her while she prepared the meal? What if instead of worrying about the preparations she had asked for *His* help? Clearly this would have been against the grain of culture in her day so I'm sure the thought would never have crossed her mind, but what if it had? What if, like Mary, she had a revelation of how culture-shattering Jesus actually was? That she really could have invited Him to be a part of this seemingly mundane task. I'm sure if Jesus were in the kitchen with Martha she, like Mary, would likely have had a revelation about Jesus that could have brought her to her knees or, it would have sparked a beautiful friendship with Jesus. Regardless, Jesus would have *loved* spending time with her there. He would have been proud of her faith in Him and how comfortable she felt inviting Him into her world, *her kitchen*, her time of preparation. Jesus came to serve, not to be served. Perhaps this is why Jesus stated that only one thing was actually *necessary* and Mary had chosen it—intimacy, time at His feet, love, honor, and closeness with Him. *Coloring outside the lines.*

CONVERSATIONS WITH GOD

Fellowship with God is our daily dialogue with Him. There's a time to be on our knees in prayer, yes, this is a critical aspect of our prayer life with Him. But our life of devotion should produce a life of consistent dialogue too. He loves it when we engage with Him amidst the "normalcy" of our day, inviting Him to be a part.

Here's something I have come to appreciate: Deep devotion produces a desire for consistent dialogue with God and consistent dialogue with God produces a desire for deeper devotion.

What many consider to be impossible, God deems possible! In fact, it's what you were created for! God wants to be part of your everyday. He says over you now, *I Am here.* He's calling out to you today, friend. God is drawing you near. Will you respond? Will you fall at the feet of the One the Father sent as our eternal Bridge to intimacy with Himself? Will you begin to see Jesus as *everything?* Will you devote your life to Him, inviting Him to be a part of your everyday?

Jesus reveals a beautiful facet of the Father's heart when He extends this very important invitation early on in His ministry. Found in Matthew 11:28, Jesus says, *"Come to Me all who are weary and burdened, and will give you rest."* This is crucial. And I believe it's what drew the women of the Bible to Jesus' feet time and time again. Their hearts responded to His invitation for intimacy, recognizing Jesus as *everything*. He was their Master. Their Healer. Their Friend. Their Savior. Their Restorer. He was mysterious and unknown, yet He was compassionate, merciful, and set out to correct the disorder of religion by restoring intimacy.

FROM THE SECRET PLACE THE ARMY ARISES

Finally, be strong in the Lord and in his mighty power. Put on the full armor of God, so that you can take your stand against the devil's schemes. For our struggle is not against flesh and blood, but against the rulers, against the authorities, against the powers of this dark world and against the spiritual forces of evil in the heavenly realms. —Ephesians 6:10-12

We dive deep into the secret place and rise up as the army of God. In spending time in God's presence, we grow strong in the Lord. We therefore *choose* to put on the armor of God available to us by His Spirit. Since our battle is not of flesh and blood, our armor is a *daily* necessity. As soldiers in the army of the Lord, we face a *daily* battle that our heart, mind, and soul needs protection from. Sometimes the arrows are aimed at us and other times the arrow is aimed at our brother or sister in Christ. Either way, we need to be ready to serve God in whatever way He needs us in any given circumstance in our everyday life.

Jesus said, "A new command I give you: Love one another. ***As I have loved you,*** *so you must love one another. By this everyone will know that you are my disciples, if you love one another."* —John 13:34-35

We are to love one another *as* Jesus loves us. In order to know how to offer that kind of love, it is imperative we spend time with

Him, in His presence, in the Word, so we experience His love first-hand and can then truly model Jesus to others, loving them as He does. What a gift He has entrusted us with friend! Demonstrating, living, modeling Christ's love *for* people *to* people.

> *From everyone who has been given much, much will be demanded; and from the one who has been entrusted with much, much more will be asked.* —Luke 12:48

Our motto as Kingdom soldiers should be that we will love the Lord our God with all our heart, mind, soul, and strength, and we will love our neighbor as we love ourselves. This kind of love is made possible in His presence. It's in His presence where His character rubs off on us and He teaches us how to love. It's in His presence, in the secret place where He reveals to you who you are in Him and His plan for your life. In His presence is where you can begin to love yourself with a pure, agape love that flows from your devotion to Him, loving Him with all your heart, all your mind, all your soul, and strength. From here you are ready to extend love to others today. The more you share, the more He entrusts you with.

> *God is love.* —1 John 4:8

What does love look like? *It looks like Jesus.* It looks like us extending grace when grace is needed. Correction when correction is needed. Kindness when kindness is needed. The list goes on. In order to determine when each is necessary, we need discernment, which we glean from our time in the presence of God, abiding in Him, in the secret place of fellowship, just you and Him. This should be your life source!

In the day and age we live, I believe that the army of God is less like an army assembled in one place as one mass unit, and more strategic positioning by the Holy Spirit. Wherever you live, you have been purposefully placed to make the greatest impact for the Kingdom of

God. You receive your marching orders from God. He guides your steps. Honor what and where Holy Spirit is prompting you to go, whom He is asking you to speak to, and what He is putting in your heart to say.

I believe Jeremiah is a picture of what the childlike can and should do through the empowerment of the Holy Spirit. God is looking for the child at heart who will trust Him with the same intensity as Jeremiah. He says over you,

> *"For I know the plans I have for you," says the Lord. "Plans to prosper you and not to harm you. Plans to give you a hope and a future."* —Jeremiah 29:11

To the younger generation He says,

> *"Do not say, 'I am too young.' You must go to everyone I send you to and say whatever I command you. Do not be afraid of them for I am with you and I will rescue you,"* *declares the Lord.* —Jeremiah 1:7-8

The Lord is reaching out His hand and touching your mouth saying to you,

> *I have put my words in your mouth.* —Jeremiah 1:9

I can hear the Lord saying now, *"Don't be afraid...you need only trust Me. I go before you. I am your rear guard. What can man say about you? What harm can they bring? For I am sending you. And I have imparted within you everything you need. Trust in Me."*

Our trust grows from our intimacy with Jesus! As we discussed in Chapter 2, the more we know Him, the more we trust Him; the more we trust Him, the deeper we know Him. It's a beautiful cycle. *It's fellowship.*

PUT ON THE ARMOR

Stand firm then, with the belt of truth buckled around your waist, with the breastplate of righteousness in place, and with your feet fitted with the readiness that comes from the gospel of peace. In addition to all this, take up the shield of faith, with which you can extinguish all the flaming arrows of the evil one. Take the helmet of salvation and the sword of the Spirit, which is the Word of God.
—Ephesians 6:14-17

In every battle, armor is necessary. We stand firm with the belt of truth buckled around our waist. Truth holds the rest of the armor together at the center, the core. The belt also holds the sword, which is the Spirit. We should be unwavering in truth, uncompromising. With intention and focus, we securely fasten truth around our waist. The truth sanctifies us and sets us apart.

Sanctify them in the truth [set them apart for Your purposes, make them holy]; Your word is truth. —John 17:17 AMP

We wear the breastplate of righteousness as redeemed sons and daughters of God. For we are the righteousness of God in Christ Jesus (see 2 Cor. 5:21) because of His blood shed on the cross, halleluiah! Our feet are fitted with the readiness that comes from knowing the gospel, which we ascertain through fellowship in His Word. Knowing the gospel, knowing what Jesus did—His death, burial, and resurrection! This fits our feet with peace enabling us to stand firm against the lies and schemes of the enemy. We will not be shaken; we will not be moved, on Christ the solid rock we stand.

He alone is my rock and my salvation, my fortress where I will not be shaken. —Psalm 62:6 NLT

We take up our shield of faith. Our unwavering faith that not only protects us from the flaming arrows of accusation from the enemy, but also completely dissolves them! The lies, the deception, the confusion will have no impact. All arrows the enemy throws at us hoping to penetrate our faith and inject doubt—no impact. Our faith in Jesus, knowing who He is and who we are because of Him, defends us from the devil's attempts.

I wear on my head the helmet of salvation, protecting my mind. As Bill Johnson puts it, we can *"think saved."* The helmet of salvation protects my mind and the renewing that is occurring through my revelation of Jesus. I'm *thinking* saved. I know who God is and who God says I am and my mind is therefore impenetrable. My mind cannot be pierced with doubt. All I can think of is Jesus. He's the author. He's the finisher of faith. As the blood of the lamb marked the doorposts during the first Passover in Egypt, protecting what was inside, so the blood of the Jesus, the Lamb of God, marks your mind the moment you are saved.

Lastly, use your sword—the sword of the Spirit. Your sword is sharp! Slicing cleanly through all deception, manipulation, and confusion of the enemy! We need the sword of the Spirit for the protection of our own minds! We should be using it daily, asking God to slice away places in us that need not be in us, separating wrong thinking from right thinking, soul and spirit, and joint and marrow.

> *For the Word of God is living and active and full of power [making it operative, energizing, and effective]. It is sharper than any two-edged sword, penetrating as far as the division of the soul and spirit [the completeness of a person], and of both joints and marrow [the deepest parts of our nature], exposing and judging the very thoughts and intentions of the heart.* —Hebrews 4:12 AMP

Here's the key with your armor: you've got to put it on and wear it. Keep it on. Remain in Him so that you continue bearing fruit (see John 15:4). Nurture your armor. As you wake up in the morning and begin your day, spend time in God's presence where you can ensure your armor is strong and hasn't been impaired. Our armor empowers us to stand firm in who we are because of who He is.

> *Finally, be strong in the Lord and in his mighty power. Put on the full armor of God, so that you can take your stand against the devil's schemes. For our struggle is not against flesh and blood, but against the rulers, against the authorities, against the powers of this dark world and against the spiritual forces of evil in the heavenly realms.* —Ephesians 6:10-12

We are to be soldiers rising up from the secret place, ready and willing for battle. We are to identify one another by the love we share and thus, the world will know Who sent us.

TAKE THE PLUNGE

A couple years ago I had this vision of a woman standing atop a mountain. Arms open wide, face lifted to the heavens. She stood tall, with her toes at the very edge of the sea cliff. I could tell by looking at her that her journey had been long and that it hadn't been easy. Yet here she stood, not a care in the world, seemingly at the end of her road with a vast ocean before her. Her hair was down and tussled loosely in the breeze. Her arms extended high above her head in total abandon. Somehow I knew: this wasn't the end of her journey—it was just the beginning. The beginning of a wild adventure she would embark upon with Jesus. God was calling her deeper. He was drawing her to His *heart*. He was challenging her to simply take the plunge. *To dive deep.* It was with joy that her arms had flung open wide from her side. With hope in her heart she trusted God and she was ready. I began to appreciate that what I was witnessing was a woman on the verge of total surrender, plunging deep into the heart of God.

As I was observing all of this, the Holy Spirit whispered simply in my spirit the words, *"Going deeper...."* I wasn't sure what to do with this at the time but as the days and months went by, I began to realize what God was showing me was a picture of myself. He was calling *me* deeper. He had drawn me to the edge of my road and was unveiling that the next step in my journey looked like this incredible plunge deep into His heart.

Going deeper...

This is when He began showing me the treasures that lie in waiting. The beautiful truths buried deep within His heart and the wild adventure at hand.

ONE FINAL QUESTION

Here is my final question as we transition into the next chapter. When was the last time you told God how much you love Him? The last time you sat down and for no reason at all uttered the words, *"I love you, God."* No hype. No agenda. No expectation. Just love for Him. I would encourage you now, wherever you are to allow those four words to flow from your heart to His, *"I love you, God."* Say it until you feel something break inside of you. Speak it until it melts away the cobwebs of a secret room in your heart. *I love, God*. A room the Father is longing to consume with His presence. A room you may never have known was there.

Abba is waiting...

What is He saying to you?

_____

_____

_____

_____

_____

_____

_____

Chapter 10

DYING TO SELF

Then he said to them all: "Whoever wants
to be my disciple must deny themselves and
take up their cross daily and follow me."
—LUKE 9:23

Our flesh could be compared to a deadly parasite living inside of us and if we feed it, it will kill us. In contrast, the Spirit inside of us gives life! And when we feed our spirits, we become more and more alive! Jesus said in John 10:10, *"The thief comes only to steal and kill and destroy but I have come that they may have life and have it abundantly"* (ESV). There *is* a way to have a full, abundant life and it's through death! Jesus died to give it to us and we die daily to live in it.

> *I have been crucified with Christ and I no longer live, but Christ lives in me. The life I now live in the body, I live by faith in the Son of God, who loved me and gave himself for me.* —Galatians 2:20

Dying to self is best demonstrated through our humility. We lay aside our own desires and plans so that Jesus can shine through us, speak through us, and *live* through us! We decide *this* day not to feed the flesh, but to feed the spirit. Prior to Christ's death on the cross this was impossible for man to do. But we've been born into a day and age in *His*-story where the Body of Christ is being established and the Holy Spirit is dispersed throughout the earth. The whole earth is filled with the glory of God as His Spirit is continually transforming His people.

We wave our white flag to the heavens, surrendering our will so that we may live our life by the influence of the Holy Spirit versus the influence of the flesh. Throughout each day we demonstrate our commitment through our choices. When we are tempted, do we give into temptation? Or do we resist the temptation? When a storm arises, do we yield to our fleshly urge of worry, anxiety, fear, or doubt? Or do we choose to trust God? Do we choose peace over worry? When our children get on our last nerve, do we give in to anger or do we allow patience to abound? Choice after choice we starve out the flesh throughout each day while feeding our spirit.

Don't get me wrong, this can be challenging. I make mistakes every day! I have a five-year-old son and a six-year-old daughter who seem to know how to push all my buttons just right! This is why, for me, I like to get up early in the morning before anyone else is awake. Get my coffee. And spend time with Abba. This is my quiet time with Him, the time when I give my day to Him, admit my need for Him, and ask Him to help me. If I learned anything, it's that I can't do it on my own! I need His life to flourish within me so that I can be more patient with my children, my husband, and even myself! I lay my heart's desires before Him, asking Him to work through me. First thing in the morning I surrender my life to Him—my mind, will, and emotions. I lay myself before Him as an offering, allowing my flesh to die and Christ to live in and through me!

Jesus had a will and therefore shows us how to overcome temptations. God led Him to the desert for 40 days and 40 nights with no food, knowing He would then be tempted by the devil. Jesus used the Word of God to overcome the enemy! There was power in Jesus' usage of Scripture because He believed every word of what He was saying. He knew the heart of God and spoke with authority as God's Son. Though His physical body was weak and hungry, His spirit was strong! He had the Holy Spirit inside of Him refreshing and strengthening His soul in His time of weakness.

Jesus taught us that when we pray, we ask God for *daily* bread. *"Give us this day our daily bread"* (Matt. 6:11). He gives us what we need each and every day to sustain us, fuel us, empower us, equip us, nourish us, and strengthen us. We don't know what lies ahead on our journey but God does. His mercies are new every morning (see Lam. 3:23). *He has fresh bread for you today.*

ABOUT THE FATHER'S BUSINESS

Did you not know that I must be about My Father's business? —Luke 2:49 NKJV

The more we are about *His* business, the less we'll be about our own! We then begin to model Jesus in our everyday life just as Jesus modeled the Father in His. So often it's in the simple things when we either represent Jesus well, or not so well (*sigh*). In our interactions with people at work, at home, church, or out at the store. Jesus came to serve and not be served (See Matt. 20:28). Jesus came to bind up the brokenhearted and set the captives free (see Luke 4:18). Jesus came to proclaim the Kingdom, to heal the sick, raise the dead, cast out demons, and cleanse the leper (See Matt. 4:23). He came with the Father's agenda tucked away in His heart, motivating His every step and His every word!

> *Very truly I tell you, the Son can do nothing by himself; he can do only what he sees his Father doing, because whatever the Father does the Son also does.* —John 5:19

Limited thinking or a faulty perception of God didn't hinder Jesus. Jesus knew how much the Father *cared* for Him. He was tuned into His Father's *voice*. He was a yielded, *surrendered vessel* walking in *fearless obedience*. Jesus was the *way* to *sonship* for us all. Every *promise* the Father has made, and would make, can be found in Him. Jesus is the *light of the world* illuminating and destroying the darkness all around Him everywhere He went. He lived His life from a place of *deep intimacy* with the Father—this was His life source while on earth—regularly tucking away to pray. Because of His death, we can also experience death to the flesh and life through the Spirit!

Does this sound familiar? I've just described Chapters 1 to 8 of this book, *Created for The Impossible*. The foundation to our death to self has been laid out and modeled for us through Jesus. We are at the point now in this book when God is saying to us; *"It's time to die."* If that offended you, then perhaps there's more religion on you than you think. Believe me, I've been there, friend! *I'm there every day* as I daily execute the tendency of the flesh, laying it down at the feet of Jesus. But it's time already; the hour of *your* crucifixion with Christ has come. Allow this to shake you to your very core. Jesus is looking to come alive in you in a fresh way today, friend, but He wants *all* of you. He wants your willingness to let go of that one final thing. Simply lay it down at His feet right now allowing your heart to follow.

> *On the road someone asked if he could go along. "I'll go with you, wherever," he said.*
>
> *Jesus was curt: "Are you ready to rough it? We're not staying in the best inns, you know."*
>
> *Jesus said to another, "Follow me."*
>
> *He said, "Certainly, but first excuse me for a couple of days, please. I have to make arrangements for my father's funeral."*
>
> *Jesus refused. "First things first. Your business is life, not death. And life is urgent: Announce God's kingdom!"*
>
> *Then another said, "I'm ready to follow you, Master, but first excuse me while I get things straightened out at home."*

Jesus said, "No procrastination. No backward looks. You can't put God's kingdom off till tomorrow. Seize the day."
—Luke 9:57-62 MSG

Essentially, Jesus is saying there's no looking back. Many of the disciples literally dropped everything immediately in response to His call. Peter and Andrew dropped their net in the water, jumped out of their boat, and with their lives said *"yes"* to Jesus' commissioning to *"Come, follow Me"* (See Matt. 4:20). The men Jesus called out to in the above passage could only give Jesus their excuses, when all He expected was their obedience. They didn't get it. They were deaf to the urgency in Jesus' commissioning and thus unfit for service in the Kingdom. We've got to make the choice to give Him our all, without delay. *If not now, when?*

TIME IS SHORT—WHO WILL YOU SERVE?

After my first encounter with God, I was overwhelmed with the revelation of how good God is, how real He is, and how big He is! I was also overwhelmed at the reality of how short time is! We no longer have time to tiptoe around who we're going to live for—*for God, or for the world?* We need to choose this day who we are going to serve (see Josh. 24:15), and continue to choose each and every day thereafter. It's a *daily* choice. Just as Jesus said in the gospels, *"Whoever wants to be my disciple must deny themselves and take up their cross daily and follow me"* (Luke 9:23). Today is the day to choose, friend: *Who will you serve?*

> I love you, My children. I made you, I created you, you are Mine. Do all that you can for me—TIME IS SHORT! The devil wants you to come home with him, I want you to come home with Me...*who will you choose?* I will give you peace, love, and happiness with eternal treasures in Heaven. The devil will give you only misery, hatred,

and grief with eternal pain in hell...*who will you choose?* I made you, I created you, I need you...*who will you choose?* Choose life not death. I love you, choose Me.

"Today I'm going to follow you Lord," should be the anthem of our heart. We deny ourselves. We follow Him. Every morning when we rise we choose Jesus. It is critical in the hour we are living that we be present minded—focused on the day at hand—but with an eternal perspective.

> *Since, then, you have been raised with Christ, set your hearts on things above, where Christ is, seated at the right hand of God. Set your minds on things above, not on earthly things. For you died, and your life is now hidden with Christ in God.* —Colossians 3:1-3

God is the author of life and Creator of the whole universe. Each day is a gift from God, friend. *"This is the day that the Lord has made, let us rejoice and be glad in it"* (Ps. 118:14 ESV). As we discussed in Chapter 7, God doesn't create without purpose. Therefore, today is filled with God's promises and with purpose; let's make the most of it by laying down our life before Him.

MY SELFISHNESS EXPOSED

I never knew just how selfish I really was until I had children. It became apparent in those first few days and weeks of my daughter's life how much I had been living for myself before she came along, shattering the world I had created for myself with her innocence and vulnerability. Suddenly, my needs came second and there was absolutely no working around that fact! My life stopped so that her life could thrive! Even the good things I wanted to do like take a shower, brush my teeth, and eat were taking a backseat in those first few weeks of motherhood! Of course as my baby got older, I was able to discover a little bit more of a balance (*you're welcome*), but to this day my kids' needs come before my own.

I'll never forget how much I wept in those early months of being a new mom. I couldn't even articulate what was happening to me, *I just cried*! Reflecting on it now, I realize I simply had no clue how selfish I was before having my baby and therefore had no way of anticipating how painful this purging of self would actually be. If I close my eyes, I can still see myself sitting there in the dark of night rocking back and forth with my beautiful newborn sleeping peacefully in my arms. I can feel my heart breaking as tears stream down my face. I can still hear my thoughts as I stared up at the ceiling silently crying out to God from the very depths of my heart, "*Why is this so hard God?! What is happening to me? What is wrong with me?!*" It's in those moments, as I've written about already, when God became even more real to me, as personal intimacy with Him was being restored. It's in these moments of self-death when my spirit began to awaken within me. It was then that I experienced a long overdue crucifixion to my flesh as my spirit came alive!

I said to my daughter just recently, "Sweetie, you brought me back to life again!" She looked at me kind of silly, "Mommy, you got *dead*?" I nodded my head and smiled, "Inside I was, yes...*but not anymore*." She flung her sweet little six-year-old arms around me as if she knew what I was talking about, and I sensed somehow she did.

This kind of death to our flesh is a constant process, which is why Jesus said we are to *die daily*. We can fight it, sure. We can buck up against it. But ultimately by fighting our death, we deny the full abundant life Jesus bought for us with His death. He died so that we could live.

JESUS DEMONSTRATES AN UNSELFISH LIFE

Christ perfectly modeled the unselfish life. The only time we really see Him asserting His own will is when He needed to get away and pray. He would send the disciples off ahead of Him so He could spend that important secret-place time with His Father, and then He'd suddenly appear with them hours later, not missing a beat. His time praying was His life source. He's showing us that *this* is the way to live! Jesus was always praying. He was consistent in dialogue with the Father. He only did as He saw His Father doing.

Jesus was about His Father's business. He served those He was sent to save. Wherever He went He healed every sickness and disease before Him. Even when He was on His way somewhere else, He would stop everything for just one person. His life was not His own, yet He walked in authority because it was His choice to live unselfishly abandoned to His Father. He *chose* to listen to the Father. He chose to heal every sick person. He wasn't a robot programmed by the Father's will. He was so full of love. He looked at the people around Him and saw a broken, lost, hurting generation. His spirit was deeply grieved. He was moved to compassion. He even wept over them.

Jesus is the picture for the life we are to live. As we are unselfishly devoted to Him, we are able to live unselfishly for others. This doesn't mean we are a doormat allowing people to walk all over us, or that we don't know how to say no to things. It means we are about the Father's business and not our own. Being crucified with Christ so now it's no longer *Krissy* who's living, it's Christ living in me! My mother-in-law always says when she meets people, she's happy if they don't remember her name. Her hope is that all they remember is *Jesus*. She is unselfish. She is about the Father's business.

What does it look like in your life to *be about the Father's business?* As I've sought the Lord, I've learned that the Father's business through me begins with my family—my children, and my husband. I can't say yes to everyone and everything else because I've said yes to them. God's heart for my walk with Him helps me to prioritize my life. There could be a hundred things that come up and I could be asked to go this way and that way, but I can only say yes to some and have to say no to others. Something I've learned over the years as life has gotten more and more full is I simply can't *do* everything. And that's OK. I'm not meant to. Saying yes to everything doesn't make one unselfish. Selflessness doesn't look like me saying yes to every person who asks for my help or invites me somewhere. Selflessness looks like my heart being motivated by the Father's will and not my own. Often we get this confused but that, perhaps, is a whole other book.

REMAIN IN HIM

I am the true grapevine, and my Father is the gardener. He cuts off every branch of mine that doesn't produce fruit, and he prunes the branches that do bear fruit so they will produce even more. You have already been pruned and purified by the message I have given you. Remain in me, and I will remain in you. For a branch cannot produce fruit if it is severed from the vine, and you cannot be fruitful unless you remain in me. Yes, I am the vine; you are the branches. Those who remain in me, and I in them, will produce much fruit. For apart from me you can do nothing. —John 14:1-5 NLT

Jesus is the grapevine and God is The Gardner. From the grapevine grow branches. When we are born again, we spring forth from the Son as a branch grows from a vine. We then begin our new life of the Spirit, leaving behind our old life dictated by the desires of the flesh.

As we remain in Him, our lives bear much fruit. As we bear fruit God, The Gardner, prunes us. He cuts from the vine any branches that are not producing fruit. It's only through our connection to the Vine, Jesus, that we bear fruit in our lives. When we remain connected to Jesus, our Father God will prune us as He sees necessary in order that our fruit will abound, grow, and mature. This pruning occurs in the secret place. It is accomplished through intimacy with God versus religious duty. It's a heart-to-heart connection.

Draw near to God and He will draw near to you. —James 4:8 NKJV

Pruning is something we allow God to do. It can be painful, yes, but it's a beautiful element of our surrendered life! We allow Him to prune away any part of us that isn't fruitful. We even allow Him to prune fruitful areas in order that we become even more fruitful. We must be open and available to Him. Vulnerable, exposed hearts freely offering our life as a willing sacrifice before Him. God prunes as He sees fit according to His purpose for us. Every branch coming from the vine has purpose and each needs to be pruned uniquely, likewise, every person has purpose and is uniquely pruned. God has His big-picture purpose at heart. We must be surrendered to Him, drawing near to Him in secret as willing, *pruneable* vessels.

God believes in you, friend. You don't have to change a thing about your personality, your looks, or your talents for God to love you and use you for His Kingdom. He just wants you to come as you are and lay yourself before Him.

Think about it—when He was forming and fashioning you in your mother's womb, He was stitching in characteristics and gifts coinciding with His plan for your life. And now as you abide in Him, you're giving Him permission to prune, nourish, mold, and shape you, developing you into the person He created you to be all along. All for His glory and His purposes for the planet!

Yet you, LORD, are our Father. We are the clay, you are the potter; we are all the work of your hand. —Isaiah 64:8

God doesn't stop forming us when we leave the womb. The difference now is we choose to offer ourselves to Him as willing vessels of clay to be ever formed by His life-shaping hands. He wants you to remain on the Potter's wheel so that He can continually shape you into the image of His Son (see Rom. 8:29). The intricacy of His hand is a reflection of the gentle, yet powerful way in which He forms, creates, and shapes life! You are His masterpiece! Willingly place yourself upon the Potter's wheel and be amazed at what He will do in and through you! *You are created for the impossible.* Since you're not yielding to a life of what is possible in your own strength, you must die to self each and every day so that Almighty God can live and work through you, deeper bringing you into those impossible dimensions of your destiny and *His*-story.

A Moment of Reflection

But the fruit of the Spirit is love, joy, peace, forbearance, kindness, goodness, faithfulness, gentleness and self-control. Against such things there is no law. Those who belong to Christ Jesus have crucified the flesh with its passions and desires. Since we live by the Spirit, let us keep in step with the Spirit. —Galatians 5:22-25

Layer by layer as we give God our all, we go deeper and deeper into His heart. Layer after layer, our flesh dissolves and our spirit arises brighter and bolder than ever. Fruit begins to spring forth in our life when we remain connected to Jesus.

This is a good place to pause for a moment with the Lord. Wherever you are right now, why don't you lie out on the floor before God and begin to cry out to Him. Give Him all of you right now—all of your heart, your mind, your soul, and your strength. It doesn't mean you're going to do it perfectly. But thankfully, Jesus is after your devotion, not your perfection.

So now, simply lay your offenses at the foot of the cross. Lay your guilt, your shame, and your burdens at His bleeding feet nailed to the cross at Calvary. See Jesus. *Behold Him.* See Him crucified. He did that for *you,* friend. He took every blow, every scoff, every spit, every joke, and every strike just to make it to the top of Calvary to bear the fullness of God's wrath for sin, for all time, *just for you*! He bore it all to pave the way so that your flesh might die *with* Him in order that your spirit can come alive by His resurrected life within you! Allow this to cut right to your heart today, friend. *Here's my life Lord.*

FINAL THOUGHT...

> *But the Lord God called to the man, "Where are you?"*
> —Genesis 3:9

God didn't ask Adam and Eve where they were because He couldn't find them. He asked them where they were because they had chosen to *hide* from Him. *Where are you?* He wanted them to acknowledge that they were hiding from Him in fear.

> *He* [Adam] *answered, "I heard you in the garden, and I was afraid because I was naked; so I hid."* —Genesis 3:10

God wants our honesty. As we've been addressing throughout this book, God cares for you, He longs to speak to you, and He longs to spend time with you, but He also wants *you. The real you.* Not the Facebook-highlight-reel you. Not the Instagram-ready you. Just *you*. He wants your honesty and transparency. God desires you, friend. Don't risk going into His presence hiding behind a façade of perfection; God sees right through that. He is fully aware of every limitation you have and what you have need of. Don't come before Him in fear, covering what you're ashamed of.

> *For we do not have a high priest who is unable to empa-*
> *thize with our weaknesses, but we have one who has been*
> *tempted in every way, just as we are—yet he did not sin.*
> *Let us then approach God's throne of grace with confi-*
> *dence, so that we may receive mercy and find grace to help*
> *us in our time of need.* —Hebrews 4:15-16

Are you ready to be honest with God about even the ugliest, scariest, most painful places in your heart? God doesn't want to condemn you; He doesn't want to judge you—*He wants to love you.* Deny yourself and give Him *you.* Bring your weaknesses to God and His strength will be made perfect in you.

Created for the impossible means leaving your old nature at the foot of the cross, dying to self daily and truly living through Christ Jesus, alive in Him bearing your new nature as a believer in your everyday life. This may seem impossible, friend, but the Holy Spirit is there to help you. Right now, allow Him to begin stirring up those areas in your life that need to die. Repent and be washed clean today. His grace will help you as you lay it all down now.

> *My grace is sufficient for you, for my power is made perfect in weakness.* —2 Corinthians 12:9

What is He saying to you?

_____

_____

_____

_____

_____

_____

_____

_____

_____

_____

_____

_____

_____

_____

Chapter 11

KINGDOM OF GRACE

But because of his great love for us, God, who
is rich in mercy, made us alive with Christ
even when we were dead in transgressions—
it is by grace you have been saved.
—Ephesians 2:4-5

"Don't you ever forget there was blood shed for you," His voice roared with a sort of crystal clear precision that seemed to slice right through my heart as I worshiped. I closed my eyes as a tear slid down my cheek. All of a sudden I saw Him stake a cross in the ground before me with such force my whole body trembled.

His Words thundered in my spirit, *"I don't want you to ever forget the cross!"* Then He spoke those original piercing words once more, but this time with greater urgency and determination, *"Don't you **ever** forget there was blood shed for you."* All I could do was weep as I nodded my head there in His presence. Still trembling, I managed to utter these few simple, yet deliberate words from my heart, *"OK, Lord, I'll never forget."*

GRACE UNDESERVED YET FREELY GIVEN

For it is by grace you have been saved, through faith—
and this is not from yourselves, it is the gift of God—
not by works, so that no one can boast. For we are
God's handiwork, created in Christ Jesus to do good
works, which God prepared in advance for us to do.
—Ephesians 2:8-10

The grace of God, His unmerited favor moving us from death to life by the blood of His Son, is quite simply *amazing*. By His grace we are saved! Not by our own works. Not by anything we can *do* or *not do*. It is purely by His grace flowing from the mercy seat of God's heart.

His grace enables us to grasp the reality of His everlasting, unconditional love for us—that He just wants us. You can look yourself in the mirror and say, "God loves me. He really loves me. *Me!* Just as I am."

He wants *you,* friend. He did all of this because He desires *you*. Everything we've discussed in this book is all woven together by the crimson thread of His love. It is by *grace* you have been saved! Rescued from death, resurrected to life with Christ, sealed by His Holy Spirit!

And you also were included in Christ when you heard the
message of truth, the gospel of your salvation. When you
believed, you were marked in him with a seal, the prom-
ised Holy Spirit. —Ephesians 1:13

His grace is such that we can now move past what we think and how we feel and simply believe what God says about us. What an amazing gift this is! By His grace I am no longer blind, *I can see*! I am no longer deaf, *I can hear*! My heart that was once broken and calloused is now whole and soft! This is grace, friend!

His grace brings us in to His chambers. It is there we become lovers of God. It's there that our heart and His heart become one. It is from there that we bear fruit! Why? Because in His presence His nature begins to take root and grow in us. The more time we spend with Him, the more He grows in us and His nature rubs off on us.

But the Holy Spirit produces this kind of fruit in our lives: love, joy, peace, patience, kindness, goodness, faithfulness, gentleness, and self-control. —Galatians 5:22-23 NLT

GOING THROUGH THE DOOR

Recently I had a vision of a door. I was standing before a closed door that unexpectedly began to open just a crack. As I reached my hand toward the knob, I realized it was my faith that had caused the door to open. Behind the door I could see light. Bright, all-consuming light filling the space beyond the door. I knew God had placed me before this door and I was to walk through it but just as I was about to, I stopped. Suddenly I was aware that in this hallway were *many* doors. For just a second a question entered my mind, *"What if* this isn't the right door for me?" And this one seed of doubt caused me to lean back, gazing down the row of doors on my right and on my left. They were all closed. There was no way to know exactly what was behind each door. So now I was posed with a question, *which door should I go through?*

What was once clear had become confusing. Why? Because I hesitated—I allowed myself to question. God began teaching me that so often this is what we do. He places us before a door that only our faith can open. We stand before our destiny and we choose to go in or remain on the outer edge. Our destiny lies within the realm of the impossible. It is there where God gets all glory for what He accomplishes through us. But we have to be willing to step through, *without fear*—fear of what He's calling us to and fear of our own limitations. Our faith opens the door to the impossible realm of our destiny, *His Kingdom*, and every step thereafter is done by faith.

This is the territory of His Kingdom where He draws all believers. This is a place where we are not bound by the limitations of this world or of our own thinking. Faith opens the door and it is by faith that we walk through it. But we can't question and we can't doubt. Sure it can be scary, but that is why we *need* faith! One faith step at a time we go through the door with Jesus into the realm of the impossible where in fact, nothing is impossible! God is stirring up a courageous heart in each of us saying, "Come on! *I Am* waiting."

LEAVE YOUR BAGGAGE AT THE DOOR

One day as I was praying, I had a similar vision about the Kingdom coinciding with the one above. It was as though I was seeing from the perspective of a child. I saw a bunch of tall *grown-ups* filling an open space. From my vantage point all I could really see was from the waist down. Focusing on the one before me, I saw a man holding a suitcase in either hand. We were all in the Kingdom of God where we were without limits yet something was holding us back. God began to reveal to me that though nothing is impossible with Him, we often bring our *own* baggage with us into the Kingdom, assigning limits to what we think God can, and will, do through us. We carry around in these suitcases our fears, our limitations, and our doubts. Our suitcase contains all of our past experiences with what is "*possible*" and "*impossible*" as documents in a filing system. One after the other we argue with what God is calling us to do based on our own limited thinking.

But God I can't do that—this document right here says I'm not qualified.

And what about this law of gravity right here? I can't walk on water...I would sink!

And this medical document right here...I can't dance upon injustice...I can't dance for freedom! I have an injured spine!

And one after the other, after the other, we apply our limitations to the limitless realm of the Kingdom! We cling to the handle of our suitcase afraid of what God will do through us if we would simply let go.

Well friend, God is saying to us today, *"Let go. It's time...I long to do the impossible through you. It's what I created you for. You're my beloved. I chose you. I know you. I placed inside of you everything you need to carry out My plan on the earth. You have yet to see what I will do through you. If you'll only let go and trust Me, you'll discover that you were indeed created for the impossible."*

> *Trust in the LORD with all your heart, and do not lean on your own understanding. In all your ways acknowledge him, and he will make straight your paths.* —Proverbs 3:5-6 ESV

It's time, friend. Will you let go? *I'm letting go!* I have decided even now as I'm writing. I am saying yes afresh and anew today! I will leave my baggage and walk through the door of the Kingdom into the realm of the impossible where I am fueled by faith and emboldened by my trust in God. I will allow hope to propel me and love to compel me! *Let's do it together!*

> *...Faith, hope and love. But the greatest of these is love.* —1 Corinthians 13:13

Hope is a key to unlocking the door. Faith causes it to open and love launches us though. Faith may open it but without love, we would never enter. Only love, love for God, love for others and love for ourselves can move us into the unknown. And it's by His grace that we have all of these things! It's by His grace that I enter the Kingdom where He sits upon His throne!

God is among us, friend! The Kingdom of God is *here,* being released throughout the earth. As the angels declared, *the whole earth is filled with God's glory!*

THE KINGDOM LOOKS LIKE...

Jesus, grilled by the Pharisees on when the kingdom of God would come, answered, "The kingdom of God doesn't come by counting the days on the calendar. Nor when someone says, 'Look here!' or, 'There it is!' And why? Because God's kingdom is already among you." —Luke 17:20-22 MSG

Jesus came to declare the Kingdom. And He died to get the Kingdom inside of you, which is *Himself.*

There was a season of my life when God dangled the image of a heart in front of me. I could see a heart and its chambers. It was the heart of God and He was showing it to me. It was as though there was something wrapped up inside the folds of His heart. *What's inside?* I would wonder, but never asked. I knew He would show me in His time. For the time being He had me studying the heart. There were four chambers. Two folds wrapped tightly around what was concealed at the core.

It's interesting that in this same season He was also saying to me, "Study the rivers that flowed from the garden." There were four rivers. And there are four chambers of a heart.

Quite simply, there were four rivers flowing from The Garden that dispensed life throughout the land. There are four chambers of the heart, which dispense life-giving blood throughout the body.

In the beginning, man was cut off from the Garden and denied access to the tree of life. Now, through Christ we are granted access to the tree of life which is Jesus Himself, we are invited to eat of His flesh and drink of His blood as we remember the price He paid on the cross. Now life flows from the Garden via the blood of Jesus flowing freely, being dispersed among the Body bringing life!

As God has unfolded all of this, He then began to open up the folds of His heart revealing what's inside, which is His Son. Jesus.

The Word. The Light. The Promise. Our Savior. Our Friend. Our Life. Grace. The Kingdom of God.

One Sunday morning I was at the altar during worship and I began asking God what the Kingdom looked like. *What is the Kingdom exactly?* And God said to me simply—it's My heart.

No, in all these things we are more than conquerors through him who loved us. For I am convinced that neither death nor life, neither angels nor demons, neither the present nor the future, nor any powers, neither height nor depth, nor anything else in all creation, will be able to separate us from the love of God that is in Christ Jesus our Lord.
—Romans 8:37-39

Nothing can separate us from God's love when we are in Christ because Christ is at the center of God's heart. Frankly, to separate us from God's love would be to rip out His very heart and no one and nothing has the power to do that.

SEEING JESUS AS *EVERYTHING*

But store up for yourselves treasures in heaven, where moth and vermin do not destroy, and where thieves do not break in and steal. For where your treasure is, there your heart will be also. —Matthew 6:20-21

Our perspective begins to shift as we begin to see Jesus as *everything*. When *He* becomes our treasure. Jesus said, "*where your treasure is, there your heart will be also.*" As we seek Him, we seek the Kingdom. Suddenly the things that once mattered so much to us before, begin to fade away. After all, *Jesus is everything!*

But seek first his kingdom and his righteousness, and all these things will be given to you as well. —Matthew 6:33

Grace must have just radiated from Jesus as rays of light radiate from the sun. Those who had need were drawn to Him. They saw *everything* in Jesus. Let's take a look at the story of Jesus visiting the home of Simon the Pharisee and what occurred when a "sinful woman" wept over Jesus' feet.

> One of the Pharisees asked Jesus to have dinner with him, so Jesus went to his home and sat down to eat. When a certain immoral woman from that city heard he was eating there, she brought a beautiful alabaster jar filled with expensive perfume. Then she knelt behind him at his feet, weeping. Her tears fell on his feet, and she wiped them off with her hair. Then she kept kissing his feet and putting perfume on them.
>
> When the Pharisee who had invited him saw this, he said to himself, "If this man were a prophet, he would know what kind of woman is touching him. She's a sinner!"
>
> Then Jesus answered his thoughts. "Simon," he said to the Pharisee, "I have something to say to you."
>
> "Go ahead, Teacher," Simon replied.
>
> Then Jesus told him this story: "A man loaned money to two people—500 pieces of silver to one and 50 pieces to the other. But neither of them could repay him, so he kindly forgave them both, canceling their debts. Who do you suppose loved him more after that?"
>
> Simon answered, "I suppose the one for whom he canceled the larger debt."
>
> "That's right," Jesus said. Then he turned to the woman and said to Simon, "Look at this woman kneeling here. When I entered your home, you didn't offer me water to wash the dust from my feet, but she has washed them with her tears and wiped them with her hair. You didn't greet me with a kiss, but from the time I first came in, she has not

stopped kissing my feet. You neglected the courtesy of olive oil to anoint my head, but she has anointed my feet with rare perfume.

"I tell you, her sins—and they are many—have been forgiven, so she has shown me much love. But a person who is forgiven little shows only little love."

Then Jesus said to the woman, "Your sins are forgiven."

The men at the table said among themselves, "Who is this man, that he goes around forgiving sins?"

And Jesus said to the woman, "Your faith has saved you; go in peace." —Luke 7:36-50 NLT

The "sinful" woman in this story saw Jesus as *everything*. She had a void in her life and was drawn to His feet. She wept over His feet, pouring out her finest perfume on Him, tears pouring from her eyes; she wiped His feet with her hair. She showed Him honor, respect, reverence, and awe! She offered Him everything because she saw everything in Him.

The man, Simon the Pharisee, whose home Jesus had been invited into, judged this woman, *and* Jesus. He couldn't fathom how Jesus was OK with such a *sinful* woman being near Him let alone touching Him and kissing His feet. Think about how radical this was for her to do! She was taking a great risk even entering the home of a Pharisee and approaching Jesus the way she did. But she knew she was safe with Jesus.

It's interesting to see the different perspectives of *sin* in this story. From the parable Jesus told about the moneylender forgiving the debts of two people, Simon acknowledged that the one having been forgiven the greater debt would be the one who would love more. Jesus used this parable to demonstrate why the woman was offering Him such affection. She had been forgiven much and therefore loved much. But here's the thing I find most interesting. It wasn't that her sin amounted to more than Simon's sin, because any sin is enough to separate us from God, it is that her *perspective* of the forgiveness available through Jesus was more accurate.

Jesus acknowledged that she had faith. And it was her faith that saved her. She saw that Jesus was everything. He was the bridge to the Father. He was the way, the truth, and the life. She judged more accurately the chasm separating her from the Father and that Jesus could mend that by offering her forgiveness. She offered Him her all and He told her she could go in peace.

It's not that Simon had *less sin* in his life than the woman. It's that he lacked an accurate perspective of sin, that sin creates a chasm between people and God. He too was in need of a Savior just as much as the woman he deemed "full of sin." If only he could seen have Jesus as everything he needed for restoration to the Father, then he too would have *loved much.*

It's not the amount of sin in our life that determines the measure of love flowing out of us—sin is sin, and we are all in need of a Savior. It's the measure of the price God paid that determines the abundance of love that flows out of us!

Seeing Jesus as everything is, well *everything*! He is our healer. Our deliverer. Our safe haven. Our refuge. Our strength. Whatever it is you have need of today, Jesus is *everything*! The grace of God is *Jesus.* Grace is the bridge between our imperfection and the perfection of God. We stand on Jesus and can walk boldly across to the Father. His grace enables us to finally acknowledge Jesus as everything.

TRANSPARENCY BEFORE GOD

As we fully understand that God receives us just as we are, we begin coming before Him more honestly. We can now be more transparent before Him about our limitations, humbly admitting our need for Him as the woman did in the story above, We can experience more peace in our lives.

"God, I need You! I can't do this without You! My anger consumes me at times, Father. Help me, Lord! I could feel pride bubbling up in me in this situation, please forgive me, Father. I admit that without You I can do nothing! But I am confident that with You all things are possible. Take this hurt from me. Remove this offense I have toward others, Abba. I need Your life to shine through me. Not my will, Your will be done this day." Some may refer to this as "self-awareness" I believe it is simply the demonstration of our death to self.

I've known people, and I've been one of them, believe me, who have come as far as being able to *admit* their own limitations but still refuse to bring them before God. I'm not even exactly sure why. Is it for fear of being exposed by God? Well, God is all-knowing. Is it for fear of God not accepting them as they are? Well, that can't be it because God *is* love. He loves us with unconditional agape love.

God is the answer to all our limitations. Whatever we have need of, whatever we need help with, we can come before Him honestly and allow Him to wash over us with grace. We need not cover in shame what God can and will restore.

Come honestly before God and allow Him to continually make you new day after day after day. Growth comes by grace, as we are transparent before Him about our weaknesses. We lay our old nature at His feet, and put on the new nature He gives us through Christ (Col. 3:5-11). Our ability to be honest before God stems from our time in His presence; it's a result of our intimacy with God. By His grace we can now bear good fruit in our lives as recipients of His great mercy and love.

> So then, since we have a great High Priest who has entered heaven, Jesus the Son of God, let us hold firmly to what we believe. This High Priest of ours understands our weaknesses, for he faced all of the same testing we do, yet he did not sin. So let us come boldly to the throne of our gracious God. There we will receive his mercy, and

we will find grace to help us when we need it most.
—Hebrews 4:14-16 NLT

HELD TOGETHER BY GRACE

What makes all of this real and relevant today is that Christ isn't dead. His bones aren't rotting in a grave. He's alive! And because He's alive, we are alive in Him! And suddenly the gap between the Kingdom of God and us is bridged and by grace we gain full access to everything He has for us as His beloved sons and daughters! *Hallelujah*! Nothing is impossible because by grace we are made strong even in our weaknesses!

> *Who then is the one who condemns? No one. Christ Jesus who died—more than that, who was raised to life—is at the right hand of God and is also interceding for us.*
> —Romans 8:34

His grace brings us into the Kingdom. As we believe, have faith, the door opens before us and we walk in. His grace empowers us to let go of everything that hinders us. Every limitation, every fear, and every doubt...we simply let go and know that God loves us and has a plan for us.

His grace frees us from striving. We can take a deep breath and recognize—*I don't have to prove myself to anyone.* By grace you are accepted unconditionally by your Heavenly Father. *God is proud of you.* He sees you and *knows* you. He created you. He made you for a very special reason and purpose in *His*-story. You were created for the impossible! You simply stand tall and walk in boldness and courage shining bright the light of Jesus, destroying the darkness around you in fearless obedience!

It is by His grace that you can ignore the lies and simply *believe* what God says about you! God thinks you can do anything, friend. Allow this truth to open your eyes and pierce your heart! Jesus takes you by the hand and walks you through your story into the Kingdom where your story and His story merge into one. Allow this powerful truth of God's grace to renew your mind today friend! *A transformation is at hand.*

What is He saying to you?

_____

_____

_____

_____

_____

_____

_____

_____

_____

_____

_____

_____

_____

_____

_____

_____

_____

_____

_____

_____

_____

_____

Chapter 12

THE RENEWED MIND: THE MIND OF CHRIST

Do not conform to the pattern of this world, but be transformed by the renewing of your mind. Then you will be able to test and approve what God's will is—his good, pleasing and perfect will.
—ROMANS 12:2

You shouldn't have said that...

Why did you put it that way?

How could you let yourself say so much?

These thoughts were racing through my mind late one night as I lay in my bed tossing and turning. Praying. Seeking God for wisdom.

Had I really messed up and said too much?

How could I have allowed myself to say those words in that particular way?

I wasn't going to allow worry to triumph, so I got up out of bed in the dark of night, closed the door to my room, and fell to my knees in the living room.

God, give me wisdom. Did I really say too much? Did I really mess up? Forgive me, Abba, for not saying that right. You know my heart and my motives. Create in me a pure heart, oh, God.

I cried out to the Father and could feel His peace settling over me. His peace that surpasses all understanding.

Still unable to go back to bed, I got up from the floor and I lay on the couch continuing to pray and seek the Lord. This issue of *saying the wrong thing* was swirling around in my mind and I could feel it taking blows at my spirit. As though it had an arm and a fist and it was just pounding on my soul. Put simply, I was beating myself up. But something about laying in the dark, alone, in the quiet, in the presence of God gave me a different perspective of what was happening.

Suddenly I thought of the scripture, *"Be alert and of sober mind. Your enemy, the devil, prowls around like a roaring lion looking for someone to devour"* (1 Pet. 5:8). The Holy Spirit then posed a question,

Where do you think the enemy prowls?

Where do you think he roars?

I thought about it for a minute. When I read that scripture, I always picture the enemy behind bushes ready to pounce on me from the outside, but suddenly I could see now that wasn't the reality. He prowls about our thoughts; his voice rises up as the voice of the accuser within our minds as it was in me this evening,

You said too much.

You messed up.

You shouldn't have said that.

The Holy Spirit then began teaching me about the lion. He said, "The enemy wants to distract you with his accusations tumbling about inside your mind, consuming your thoughts. But, as a child of God, Jesus—*the Lion of the Tribe of Judah*—has made His home within you and His roar is louder than that of the accuser! Stop allowing the enemy to roar in your mind and declare that the roar of Christ in you is stronger! If you'll stop entertaining the accuser, you'll realize he is not a lion at all. His roar isn't anything more that the mere cry of one who has been defeated!"

Immediately, I rose up from the couch and I began declaring over my mind, "The Lion within me is stronger! His voice is louder! Greater is He who is in me than He who is in the world! I believe what God says about me. He doesn't need me to be perfect. Jesus is perfect!" I could feel Christ swelling up within me. I could sense as His roar silenced the mere yelp of the defeated one. Suddenly I felt strong again. I felt peace. I was encouraged. I had demolished the lie of the enemy with the truth making my thoughts obedient to Christ!

THE BATTLEGROUND

The weapons we fight with are not the weapons of the world. On the contrary, they have divine power to demolish strongholds. We demolish arguments and every pretension that sets itself up against the knowledge of God, and we take captive every thought to make it obedient to Christ.
—2 Corinthians 10:4-5

Our mind can be a war zone! At conflict are the narratives spoken over us throughout our life. They war in our mind over our identity. There are the lies the enemy has told us about who we are versus the truth of who God says we are. Which side wins is up to us. It's whichever narrative we choose to believe. Confusion can cause us to teeter back and forth between the two but at the end of the day it's whichever side we spend the most time entertaining that will win.

Here's a question: when you are faced with insecurity regarding who you are or what you're called to, where do you go? What you do when you're experiencing doubt is very important. Do you sit in front of the television quietly longing to find affirmation through a character on your favorite show? Do you call a friend? Do you spend time in prayer? *What do you do?*

It's important for us to be strategic in our battles. There is no need for us to entertain the lie when we've been given the authority to take captive *every* thought and make it obedient to Christ! Take prisoner every idea that would cause you torment, anxiety, worry, shame, guilt, regret, and so on. You have been given power over your thoughts by the blood of Jesus. When the war is raging in your mind, bring your battle to the foot of the cross.

If you have been wounded, rest your head against the chest of Abba in the secret place, allowing the rhythm of His heart to beat life back into your soul. Let Him whisper words of truth, reinforcing the narrative *He's* spoken over you since you were in the womb. Allow Him to remind you who you are and *whose* you are. You will find that the battle ends quickly because your enemy has already been defeated. You will be reminded that you hold the keys to victory and your perspective will shift from battle-scared victim to blood-bought victor!

No, in all these things we are more than conquerors through him who loved us. —Romans 8:37

Jesus Won the Victory Over Our Mind

"Father, if you are willing, take this cup from me; yet not my will, but yours be done." An angel from heaven appeared to him and strengthened him. And being in anguish, he prayed more earnestly, and his sweat was like drops of blood falling to the ground. —Luke 22:42-44

A great victory occurred in the Garden the night before Jesus was crucified. Blood was shed in the very dust that man was created from through the agony of the Son as He cried out to God, *"Father, if you are willing, take this cup from me!"* Yet as excruciating as the Father's will was, in agony—Jesus relented, *"Nevertheless, not my will, but yours, be done"* (NKJV). As the angel of the Lord tended to Him, sweat like drops of blood fell into the dust of the earth there in the Garden.

A major triumph occurred this night—*victory over the will.* Jesus had been given free will just as we are. He had the opportunity to *choose* to follow God and carry out His will just as we do. He walked through many temptations in His time on earth, but no temptation was as excruciating as the night before His crucifixion when He pleaded with the Father to take the cup from Him. It's possible that the Father would even have honored the Son's plea had Jesus not yielded His will to the Father. *"Nevertheless, not my will, but yours be done."*

God created us all with a free will. As we discussed in Chapter 3, the best thing we can do with our will is to surrender it to the One who gave it to us. But we need to be intentional about this. Surrendering our will is a critical element in our walk with God. We live this life by faith not by sight.

Even though He was in torment, Jesus still resolved in His heart to carry out the covenant He had made with the Father before the very foundations of the earth were even formed. The blood of Jesus was shed there in the dust as massive clots came seeping from His pores while, in anguish, He passionately poured out His heart there in the Garden.

> *For he chose us in him before the creation of the world to be holy and blameless in his sight. In love he predestined us for adoption to sonship through Jesus Christ, in accordance with his pleasure and will.* —Ephesians 1:4-5

I believe this is the place where the victory over our mind was won. Yes, Jesus walked in victory daily and as we saw in the dessert when he was tempted by satan, he overcame; but there is something so profoundly powerful yet simple that happens here in tThe Garden. Jesus submits His own personal will to the will of the Father. We are able to see just how strong human will can be that it would cause even the Son of God to ask the Father if He'd be willing to alter His eternal plan.

We can't take lightly the power of our will and our ability to choose. This is why dying daily is so important! We need to be intentional in taking up our cross daily to follow Christ, yielding to the Father's will and not our own.

USE YOUR TOOLS

One Sunday morning while at the altar kneeling and worshiping and praying, head bowed, I felt someone walk up beside me and put their hand on my back. It was a man's hand and it was warm. But instead of allowing them to just pray for me, I felt a sense of urgency to lift my head and turn quickly to look. There was no one there. Literally, all around me was wide-open space as most people were standing at their seats. *I sensed it was Jesus.* Bowing my head again I simply responded, *"Yes Lord?"* He said to me, "I've placed a toolbox beside you." As His Words echoed in my spirit, a vision of Jesus walking up beside me, leaning down with His left hand on my back and His right hand placing a toolbox next to me unfolded in my spirit. *"Thank you Lord."*

Imagine the Bible as your toolbox and the principles within are the tools needed in building the life God has marked out for you. Each tool is unique to the unique scenarios we face each and every day.

Today I may be experiencing worry. If so I can recall the teachings of Jesus in Matthew 6 about worry and how to overcome. Thanks to the Holy Spirit within me I can recall these scriptures anytime I need them because they are stored in my heart and alive in my spirit. When I'm feeling weak, I'm reminded that Christ is made strong in my weakness; and so it goes. I believe that these beautiful principles are the *heavenly treasures* Jesus is talking about in Matthew.

Do not store up for yourselves [material] treasures on earth, where moth and rust destroy, and where thieves break in and steal. But store up for yourselves treasures in heaven, where neither moth nor rust destroys, and where thieves do not break in and steal; for where your treasure is, there your heart [your wishes, your desires; that on which your life centers] will be also. —Matthew 6:19-21 AMP

Jesus paints a beautiful picture for us here. Heavenly treasures cannot be stolen; they will never rust or decay or lose their value. They are the *principles* of Heaven that Jesus released upon the earth for us to use as tools for our life! *Yes*! This is what I stockpile! This is what I value and thus what my heart will pursue! Thank you God for fresh heavenly treasures that I can draw on anytime I need them! The enemy doesn't know what you have up your sleeve when your treasures are stored in Heaven! He has no access there!

CONFUSION

For God is not the author of confusion but of peace
—1 Corinthians 14:33 NKJV

The enemy will try to confuse your purpose and your identity. He'll try to confuse the very word God gave you. He quotes scripture you know. He takes truth and perverts it for selfish gain. He uses the Word of God to confuse the promise of God for your life.

We know the Bible says, *"Resist the devil, and he will flee from you"* (James 4:7). But *how* do we resist him? We resist him by *knowing* the truth. By refusing to believe the lie and holding fast to the truth of God's Word. We must remain in the truth. Being rooted and grounded in truth is to have a firm foundation in truth! In a culture where everything is deemed relative, we need to stand unwavering. There *is* absolute truth, friend, and it's in every word God has spoken.

Jesus is the Son of God. He is the Word made flesh. Jesus *is* Truth.

Our faith needs to be rooted in this reality. If we waver on this, we give a foothold to the enemy to expand our doubt, creating a chasm between God and us once again. Doubt welcomed sin in the beginning creating separation between God and us. Don't allow the enemy to sow seeds of doubt into your mind, friend. We need to be settled on this reality as the unified Body of Christ: the Word of God is absolute. The Bible is absolute truth. Jesus confirmed this, end of story!

God wants to renew our mind while the enemy wants to pollute our mind through deception, manipulation, and fear. He gets us wrapped up in confusion when God wants to wrap us in a warm blanket of truth.

Confusion feeds on itself. If you allow yourself to be confused, you'll only get more confused until you're *so* confused you don't even know where and how the problem started. You roll around in the mud of confusion so long you can't remember what the root of the problem was. Confusion is like sinking sand. If we step in it and don't pull our foot out right away, we get stuck and we don't know how to make our way back. Confusion is birthed in us when we allow ourselves to believe a lie from the enemy. As we entertain the lie, it grows. But truth smashes through the lie. Allow truth to come crashing through today, friend!

A HEALING WORD

Slicing right through my confusion thundered the voice of God! His voice was like the waters. Unmistakable. I had never heard it before but I knew Him when I heard Him. I was 14 years old and had just fallen to my knees desperate to hear from God. Confusion consumed my mind. I had lost all sense of who I was. For the last few years, I had gotten caught up in a whirlwind of self-doubt and self-loathing, and had absolutely no idea who I even was anymore. I had had enough! And for the first time in my life, in the middle of a noisy youth convention with hundreds of teenagers singing and dancing around me to the worship music blaring from the platform, I dropped to my knees and cried out to God.

Who am I God?!

Please, tell me!

Who am I?!

Suddenly it was just me and God—*and He spoke*. His voice was clear and it cut right through the chaos of my mind. His message so uncomplicated yet life defining. He said to me, "Krissy, eagles fly alone." His Words saturated my mind with peace, purpose, identity, and love. Suddenly I could see one lone eagle soaring high above the tops of beautiful snow-covered mountains. The eagle soared with elegance. It appeared at peace and without a care in the world. I could see that the eagle didn't need a flock of other birds around it to feel valuable. The eagle knew its purpose. The eagle was functioning just how it was created to function—without limits, without hindrance. It was soaring above all the noise, and all the hustle and bustle of the earth below. And it was content.

"Eagles fly alone."

That's all He said, but the message He communicated was clear and eternal. He spoke a healing word that continues speaking volumes to me to this day. With His Word came life more abundant! His Word brought peace, purpose, and identity to a broken teenager desperate for clarity. Suddenly everything made sense.

Though it seemed impossible to ever climb up out of the chaos roaring through my mind, I'm created for the impossible. And with just one word I was finally free to *soar*. I believed what God said about me that day, even though I didn't fully understand it all then, I chose to believe Him. I've clung to that word in the 20 years since He spoke it and it's more alive to me today than ever!

God's Word is eternal! His voice slices right through the confusion with a message of absolute truth. God has a word for you today too, friend. What are you confused about? What do you need God to show you? Whatever it is, bring it before Him now. Pause for a moment, just you and God; cast your cares at His feet and *listen*. He has a healing word of truth for you.

> *Then they cried to the Lord in their trouble, and he saved them from their distress. He sent out his word and healed them; he rescued them from the grave. Let them give thanks to the Lord for his unfailing love and his wonderful deeds for mankind.* —Psalm 107:19-21

WHAT IS TRUTH?

> *If you hold to my teaching, you are really my disciples. Then you will know the truth, and the truth will set you free.* —John 8:31-32

On the day of Jesus' crucifixion, Pilate asked Jesus a very important question. With Jesus standing before him having already been beaten and bruised, Pilate looks Him square in the eye and asks, *"What is truth?"* (John 18:38).

It's interesting that Pilate doesn't wait for Jesus to answer. It's as though something in the eyes of Christ satisfies the question. Whether Pilate realized it or not, the answer to his question was looking right at him. Pilate immediately went out to the Jews who had gathered against Jesus and reports, *"I find no basis for a charge against him"* (John 18:38).

What is truth?

I believe this is a question we are still asking ourselves in today's worldly culture. Truth is being called into question, beaten, mocked, taken for granted, and persecuted. Truth is on display for the world to mock. Truth is being taken out of our schools and tossed in the mud to be trampled on by the systems we've created by our own interpretation of what we think *truth* really is.

Jesus boldly declares the answer to our question in John 14:6, *"I am the way and the truth and the life. No one comes to the Father except through me."* Jesus is Truth.

Imagine you are standing at a crossroad and need to find the way but the sky is dark. You cannot see which path you should take. But suddenly Jesus comes as the light illuminating the path before you. He extends His hand to you and says, "I Am the way, the Truth, and the Life. I am here to lead you to the One whom you are searching for. Come follow me, and I'll take you right to Him."

We either believe Jesus or we don't. We either believe the Word, or we don't. There isn't a middle road. There's light or there's darkness. If we believe God we believe His Word.

Jesus Christ is the same yesterday and today and forever.
—Hebrews 13:8

God is not a man, that He should lie. —Numbers 23:19
NKJV

We need to be resolved in our conclusions about God. The apostles concluded that they were *convinced* about the gospel. They didn't just believe. They had made conclusions in their hearts and were resolute in the reality of the Father, Son, and Holy Spirit; about the Kingdom of God and the Gospel of Christ Jesus our Lord. Our conclusions should leave no room for doubt. Be decisive. *Jesus is...Jesus said...God is...God said...*His Word is absolute.

Our culture today says everything is relative. And my generation seems to be leading the way in this message. What is right for me may be wrong for you and vice versa. I'm not wrong, you're not wrong. But for us to be absolute in everything being relative is a contradiction in and of itself!

Clearly there is truth! And it's time we stand on it and for it. The Word of God will never contradict itself. It is its own defender. Know the Word and the Word will know you. Live in the Word and the Word will live in you. Trust the Lord and the Lord will trust you.

In a world that's boldly proclaiming what's relative, we as believers should boldly proclaim what is Truth!

Then you will know the truth and the truth will set you free. —John 8:32

Created for the impossible means we can live in the world but not be conformed by the world. We can be surrounded by relativism and doubt but not be swayed in our stand for truth. Day in and day out we can be transformed by the renewing of our minds in Christ Jesus. We can love those who hate us and we can be overwhelmed by peace in a world riddled with worry and fear. *Why?* Because God said so, and we are a people who believe what God says.

Did God Really Say

He said to the woman, "Did God really say, 'You must not eat from any tree in the garden'?" —Genesis 3:1

In the beginning, the enemy plants the first seed of doubt with the question, *"Did God really say?"* What a strategy he used to get Eve to eat of the tree by creating this broad view of what God said or didn't say, "Did God *really say* you couldn't eat from *any* of the trees in the garden?" I can imagine her thoughts as she replied, "Well, no, He said we could eat of all the trees except for that *one.*" Now suddenly eating from that one doesn't seem like such a big deal compared to the suggestion he planted that she couldn't eat from *any* of the trees.

This is what the enemy does. He takes what is absolute and perverts it as being up for interpretation. *Did God really say?*

We need to be like Jesus was when He was confronted with the devil's manipulative schemes. Declaring, "Depart from me Satan!" Any word that calls into question the Word of God should cause us to say: *Enough!*

The enemy sows seeds of doubt, fear, and deception into our minds making us uncertain about what God really *meant.* The enemy is happy if he can get you to question God's intention behind His Word instead of just taking Him at His Word.

In the Garden the enemy deceived Adam and Eve's mind. He placed a proverbial question mark where God had left a period. "Did God really say?" Eve hadn't even fathomed another option beyond what God commanded until the enemy came slinking into the Garden posing the question.

Don't allow the enemy to insert a question mark into your story where God has placed a period, or even an exclamation point! God's Word is His Word. God's promises are *yes* in Christ. Simply give His yes your *amen* as you resolve to agree with and believe what God says about you.

Right now close your eyes and declare over your life an absolute, concrete truth, demolishing the enemy's question mark with God's exclamation point. Proclaim from the depths of your heart, "YES, God really said!"

WE ARE TRANSFORMED

This is when the transformation begins. As we boldly declare the word as truth. As we stand upon His Word knowing it's a firm foundation. Refusing to conform to the patterns of this world. Refusing to believe the deception the enemy spews through today's culture. We are to be anchored in truth, rooted and grounded in love.

Suddenly the reality of who God is , His will for our life, and who He says we are becomes alive in us and through us! I realize, I'm no longer a *slave to fear*—I'm alive in Christ. I'm a new creation. I can do all things through Christ who gives me strength. Jesus wins! I am a victor not a victim. The lens we see the world through changes as our minds are renewed through the fresh perspective of Christ Jesus who is alive in us! When we look in the mirror we see a daughter...a son. We see life…hope…peace…joy. We begin to bear much fruit and are truly transformed in the image of Christ through the renewing of our mind!

The transformation through the renewed mind occurs as we allow God to wash us in truth. As we believe what God says about us versus what the enemy says. When we conclude that the Word of God is absolute. As we believe that God's Word is unchanging and unwavering, then we too become unwavering and unwilling to believe any word that would confuse the absolute Word of God.

Created for the impossible means we are so wrapped up in truth, no matter what comes our way we will not be shaken. The storms of life may rage against us at times but we stand upon a firm foundation of truth and will not be intimidated, knocked down, or rattled. God is for us, who then can come against us? Speak this over yourself right now, friend. "God is *for* me, who can be against me." Allow the Lion within you to roar! Allow that voice of truth to slice through any negative thoughts that contradict the wisdom and knowledge of who God is and who He says you are. And finally, allow the mind of Christ to renew your mind and transform your life as you set your thoughts on things above, where Christ is seated, and your treasures are hidden. *God thinks you can do anything.*

> *Since, then, you have been raised with Christ, set your hearts on things above, where Christ is, seated at the right hand of God. Set your minds on things above, not on earthly things. For you died, and your life is now hidden with Christ in God.* —Colossians 3:1-3

What is He saying to you?

PART 4

Believe What God Says About You

Chapter 13

GOD THINKS YOU CAN DO ANYTHING

*And if the Spirit of him who raised Jesus from
the dead is living in you, he who raised Christ
from the dead will also give life to your mortal
bodies because of his Spirit who lives in you.*
—ROMANS 8:11

It was 4 A.M. and I was making my way from the kitchen to the living room trying not to spill my coffee as I carefully stepped over toys scattered about the pathway to the couch. Taking small sips of my coffee as I tiptoed through my house, I watched as the soft moon beams gently danced around the floor. I remember I had just made it to the edge of my couch when I heard Him. That sweet whisper of the Holy Spirit speaking a good morning word to my spirit, *"God thinks you can do anything,"* He said; and I stopped. I didn't want to move.

I gently lowered my coffee cup from my mouth and closed my eyes. I heard Him say it again, this time a little louder, *"God thinks you can do anything."*

Standing there in the dark, I recalled where and when I had heard this before. It was two years prior at a service with Marilyn Hickey. She had been speaking about finding Jesus in every book of the Bible and midway through her message she stopped, looked out at the crowd and, as if speaking right to me, said this statement that pierced right through to the core of my heart, *"God thinks you can do anything."*

Her tone was casual and her demeanor matter of fact, sort of an *"oh, by the way—God thinks you can do anything."* And then she continued on with her message. But I never forgot that. And now here in the early morning hours, the Holy Spirit was whispering these piercing *oh-by-the-way* words again in my spirit to remind me, *God thinks you can do anything.*

BELIEVE WHAT GOD SAYS ABOUT YOU

I tell you the truth, if you had faith even as small as a mustard seed, you could say to this mountain, "Move from here to there," and it would move. Nothing would be impossible."—Matthew 17:20 NLT

As remarkable as all of this is, I think the most extraordinary thing about it is that *I actually believe Him!* I believe that when God interrupts my early morning walk from my kitchen to my couch, not waiting for me to sit down, so that He can say to me, "Hey Krissy—I think you can do anything," that He's right! *I can.* And the reason I *know* I can is because He says I can.

Romans 8:11 says that the same Spirit that raised Christ from the dead lives in me! And Romans 8:31 says if God is for me who can be against me? And Romans 8:37 says that I am more than a conqueror in Christ Jesus! I've got the Word backing up the promise! And God is not a man that He should lie (see Num. 23:19)! So there you have it friend, when God says to me, *"Krissy, I think you can do anything."*

He's not looking for argument or debate; He's looking for my faith and trust as I simply *believe what He says about me.*

Friend, God thinks *you* can do anything! He knows it! He went through great lengths to make impossible things possible! Ripping open eternity, He sent His Son into this earth so that He could make His home in your heart, empowering you to do all things through Him! *It's time for you to believe!*

Another thing God has been teaching me is that I don't need to have perfect faith, just a drop will do. Just a drop can move mountains! Just a drop can part seas and cause me to walk atop the impossible! Just a drop is enough faith for me to believe what He says about me. *Just a drop will do.*

What if it really were that simple? That all we need to do is simply *believe.* That all we need is a drop of faith. *What if...?* Well, the case is closed friend. It *is* that simple.

> *Yet to all who did **receive** him, to those who **believed** in his name, he gave the right to become children of God— children born not of natural descent, nor of human decision or a husband's will, but born of God.* —John 1:12-13

Jesus came to unravel the complicated mess humanity had made of things. He came to draw all men unto Himself. He came with a simple message of hope for all humanity: just receive Him and believe in His name and you will be welcomed into the family of God.

His blood, not our works, is the glue forever bonding us to the family of God. Our works can actually blind us from what we already have, causing us to run and run and run like hamsters in a wheel never actually getting anywhere. We expend all this energy and for what? We haven't made any progress. We end up exhausted without ever getting anywhere with just the illusion of progress. We're so busy running and running and running we end up blind to those who are hurting around us who we should be stopping to help. We need to allow the Holy Spirit to take the blinders off opening our eyes to the reality around us.

There's a whole world out there—mountains to climb, seas to part, and people to encourage. There's a whole ocean we are called to walk on. What are we doing inside of this wheel when we could be out there in our destiny? The destiny God wrote out for us in His-story.

When we finally realize we've been running and never actually progressing, take a deep refreshing breath and simply step out of the wheel...

We step out of the boat...

We climb out of the box...

We color outside the lines...

God has called us to a life without borders. He's called us to run and not grow weary, to walk and not faint. He says, *"I have wings for you."* He's called us to soar high above the chaos of the world with a heavenly vantage point. We are to have a *Jesus perspective,* which is to think higher and dream bigger. We are to rest in His Word and His promises. No more striving. No more running around in hamster wheels or spinning our tires. Just perfect peace...soaring with Jesus, breaking every hindering thought, believing what God says about us, exchanging the lies for the truth. That's what faith *is.* It's believing what God has spoken more than what you can see! *"Without faith it is impossible to please God"* (Heb. 11:6). Friend, you have been given the authority to ignore the enemy and believe God.

> *As the heavens are higher than the earth, so are my ways higher than your ways and my thoughts than your thoughts.*
> —Isaiah 55:9

WHAT A GIFT: THE HOLY SPIRIT

I have much more to say to you, more than you can now bear. But when he, the Spirit of truth, comes, he will guide you into all the truth. He will not speak on his own; he will speak only what he hears, and he will tell you what is yet to come. He will glorify me because it is from me that he will receive what he will make known to you. All that belongs to the Father is mine. That is why I said the Spirit will receive from me what he will make known to you. —John 16:12-15

Just as Jesus is a bridge between the Father and us, the Holy Spirit is a bridge connecting us to the fullness of the Godhead. With the Holy Spirit living in us, we are connected to the Vine that is Christ, and have ears to hear what the Father is saying because Holy Spirit only communicates what He hears from the Father. It's a phenomenal thing, friend. We need the Holy Spirit in our life, consuming our heart, refreshing our soul, and transforming and renewing our mind.

God desires that we have intimacy not just with Himself, not just with His Son, but also that we have true, intimate relationship with Holy Spirit! This is a beautiful facet of Himself that so many of us neglect in our day-to-day lives yet this was the very facet of God that Jesus was so excited to give us as His gift!

*But now I am going to him who sent me. None of you asks me, 'Where are you going?' Rather, you are filled with grief because I have said these things. But very truly I tell you, it is for your good that I am going away. Unless I go away, the Advocate will not come to you; but if I go, **I will send him to you**.* —John 16:5-7

Jesus was eager to return to the Father in order to release to you this special gift! Because with the Holy Spirit inside us, there is nothing we can't do in Jesus' Name! Even greater things will we do through the Name of Jesus by the power of the Holy Spirit living within us!

Very truly I tell you, whoever believes in me will do the works I have been doing, and they will do even greater things than these, because I am going to the Father. And I will do whatever you ask in my name, so that the Father may be glorified in the Son. You may ask me for anything in my name, and I will do it.—John 14:12-14

Nothing is impossible! The Holy Spirit is our helper. He helps us hear the voice of God, see ourselves as God sees us, and walk in victory over the wiles of the enemy! No weapon formed against us can prosper! He is a seal upon our hearts of our adoption as sons and daughters! By Him we cry *Abba*, Father!

> *And because we are his children, God has sent the Spirit of his Son into our hearts, prompting us to call out, "Abba, Father."* —Galatians 4:6 NLT

I used to wonder why Jesus would say it is *for our good* that He would leave to be with the Father. What could be better than God Himself in human form walking among us, teaching us, and modeling firsthand how to live for God in our everyday life? Really, what or rather *who* could be better?

> *But when the Father sends the Advocate as my representative—that is, the Holy Spirit—he will teach you everything and will remind you of everything I have told you.* —John 14:26 NLT

You've been given the blood-bought gift of the Holy Spirit, friend. God sends us His Spirit as a gift on behalf of the Son. Imagine a present that is beautifully wrapped in shimmering gold paper with flecks of jasper and ruby and a big crimson-red bow with a note marked, "TO: *(insert your name)* FROM: Your Abba, Father." And when you open it up, the breath of God releases over you and Holy Spirit bursts inside of you as a flame of fire! The same Spirit that raised Christ from the dead now lives in you as a gift from the God delivered through the blood of His Son. You are filled with supernatural power from Almighty God and nothing and no one can come against you!

> *Now he is exalted to the place of highest honor in heaven, at God's right hand. And the Father, as he had promised,*

gave him the Holy Spirit to pour out upon us, just as you see and hear today. —Acts 2:33 NLT

What a gift the Holy Spirit truly is! Through Him our eyes are open to the truths contained in Scripture. The mysteries of God are revealed through Him. The eyes of our hearts are opened and our ears can finally hear! There is much more that Jesus wanted to reveal to His disciples but they couldn't bear it at the time. Without the infilling of the Holy Spirit, there was no way they could handle all that was to be unveiled. It wasn't until after the resurrection and Jesus ascended to Heaven that the disciples went to the upper room praying and waiting for ten days for Holy Spirit to come that they were then able to bear the fullness of truth that would be revealed to them.

The product of that infilling is what we find throughout the Book of Acts and the epistles. The revelations and teachings that came to the Apostles, the miracles, signs, and wonders that followed the preaching of the gospel were all products of the Holy Spirit operating through the men and women of God. What an extraordinary gift Holy Spirit is! Ordinary men and women doing extraordinary things through the power of the Spirit of God at work within them, and through them!

> *But you will receive power when the Holy Spirit has come upon you; and you shall be my witnesses both in Jerusalem, and in all Judea and Samaria, and to the ends of the earth."*—Acts 1:8

We need the Holy Spirit in our lives, friend! If we don't have Him, we are missing out on an instrumental facet of God! The very facet Jesus died to bring us. Think about it. The Bible says, *"For the joy set before Him He endured the cross"* (Heb. 12:2). He endured death knowing He would be releasing life to all who would believe! He went through hell on the cross so He could give us Heaven! Both the Father *and* the Holy Spirit abandoned the Son on the cross (see Mark

15:34), left Him all alone to bear the full punishment of sin upon Himself so that we would never have to be alone again!

This was His joy: knowing that you would soon be equipped to live an abundant life—life filled with His Spirit inside of you helping you from the inside out. The impossible now becomes possible: humanity living lives that are pleasing to God because of the fruit we bear through His spirit inside of us as we lives as branches connected to the vine (see John 15:4).

> *But the fruit of the Spirit is love, joy, peace, forbearance, kindness, goodness, faithfulness, gentleness, and self-control.*
> —Galatians 5:22-23

He would send us this precious gift from the Father, the Holy Spirit, to live inside of us restoring us to relationship with His Father, *our Father*. He knew this was the only way. His blood shed on the cross made it possible for Holy Spirit to make a home inside of our hearts!

I love what Jesus says to Mary when she discovers He has risen from the grave, *"Don't cling to me,"* Jesus said, *"for I haven't yet ascended to the Father. But go find my brothers and tell them, 'I am ascending to my Father and your Father, to my God and your God'"* (John 20:17 NLT). He declares that now God is not only *His* Father, but He's *her* Father and the disciples' Father! He sends her off to *go*, and *tell*. Hallelujah!

Where once man could not come into the presence of God at all because they were unclean, now, by the blood of Jesus, not only can we come near, but God now makes a home in our hearts by His Spirit and lives inside all who believe.

> *Jesus answered him, "If anyone loves me, he will keep my word, and my Father will love him, and we will come to him and make our home with him."* —John 14:23 ESV

CREATED FOR THE IMPOSSIBLE

Throughout this book we have been on a journey. This journey was very intentional. First, we were challenged to believe that God cares for us. This is the very foundation. Realizing that we are not just a number to Him. We are not just one in a billion. We are *one*. *The one*. The one He sent His Son for. The one He created the earth for. The one He runs to with wide-open arms when we return home. The one Jesus makes intercession for at the right hand of God. The one whose hairs are numbered. The one who was pardoned for purpose. The one whose heart He abides in. Created for the impossible means believing that God cares for us.

Next we explored the way He speaks. His life-giving, purpose-restoring voice through the intimate fellowship He desires with you, His beloved. His voice that longs to speak right to your heart, restoring the intimacy and fellowship He sent His Son to die for. Created for the impossible means believing that God speaks to us, and tuning into hear His voice.

We discussed the power and importance of our surrender. Giving God our all. Willingly laying our lives down at the feet of Jesus, giving Him the reward of His suffering. That the most important thing we can do with the free will God has given us is *choosing* to yield to the will of the Father. Created for the impossible means surrendering our will to Him in total abandon.

This leads us to become more fearless as we dare to step out atop the waters of the impossible with Jesus. Locking eyes with Him. Trusting that He holds our destiny in His hands. Trusting that though the winds and the waves may be swelling up around us, our eyes are fixed on Jesus—what harm can come against us? Created for the impossible means stepping out in obedience without fear, launched by love, trusting God with every step!

We discovered the simple truth of the cross. The way has been made for us. Jesus' blood covers us and now all can come near to the Father! We are restored to fellowship with God as He originally created humanity to be. Created for the impossible means accepting God's gift of salvation, being washed white as snow by the crimson blood of the spotless Lamb of God, *Jesus.*

We come boldly before the throne of grace welcomed with open arms into the family of God as His beloved children. Slicing through the doubt and chaos of our mind is this beautiful message from the heart of God for you, *"You're my beloved."* Created for the impossible means being a child of God and truly embracing our identity as His child. Gazing into the mirror seeing a *daughter…*a *son.*

From here our purpose unfolds. We realize that God has written our story weaving our story with His-story. We walk with promise and His promise is His Word. His Word has power and He places His Word in our mouth to call even the dead things around us to life! Created for the impossible means that like Ezekiel, we call out to the dead bones and dead hearts among us, *"Come alive!"*

We see that we were created to shine Jesus to the lost and dying world around us. We are the light of the world and that light has the power to destroy the darkness. We shine bright the resurrection power and authority of Christ showing that there's hope for the world, which is Christ in you. Created for the impossible means choosing not to hide our light but allowing it to shine with joy and love for the entire world to see!

From here we take the plunge deep into the secret place with God. Excavating the treasures of His heart. Picking up the truths buried there in the soil below His ocean of love for us. We make our home there in His heart and He too makes His home in ours. We dive deep into the secret place and rise up as the army of God, strategically placed and wearing the full armor of God. Created for the impossible means plumbing the depths of God's heart, choosing intimacy with Him daily.

We therefore die to self, while walking in humility, yielded to the Father's plan each and every day. We are crucified with Christ so it is no longer we who live but Christ living in and through us. Created for the impossible means choosing to take off the old nature and put on the new nature in Christ Jesus.

His grace is sufficient and His power is made strong in our weakness. His grace empowers us to do all things. It's by His grace that we can believe what God says about us. It is by grace we are saved! Created for the impossible means living life through grace knowing that salvation was God's gift to us through Christ Jesus, not by our works.

With the renewed mind of Christ we begin to think healthier, winning the battle for the mind because the blood that Jesus shed provides a path for victory over our will! Jesus won over the mind. Created for the impossible means we can live in the world but not be like the world, that we can be transformed by the renewing of our mind in Christ Jesus!

GOD THINKS YOU CAN DO ANYTHING

Heal the sick, raise the dead, cleanse those who have leprosy, drive out demons. Freely you have received; freely give. —Matthew 10:8

And now, here we are. We are ready to stand in the reality that we can do all things through Christ who gives us strength. With His Spirit at work inside of us we can truly live where we are planted. We can remain in Him and bear much fruit in our lives. We don't need to wait for tomorrow to come, we can make a difference today. We heal the sick, raise the dead, love the unlovely, cleanse the leper, have joy in parenting, drive out demons, show patience to our children, show kindness and goodness to a stranger, and walk in faithfulness, gentleness, and self-control in our everyday lives. With our family, in our workplace, at the grocery store—wherever the day leads us, we are walking as ambassadors for Christ!

*We are therefore Christ's ambassadors, as though God were
making his appeal through us.* —2 Corinthians 5:20

Now, as you identify those thoughts that have held you back, you can finally begin to believe what God has been saying about you all along! He thinks you can do anything! Take your drop of faith and use it to move mountains—mountains of doubt, mountains of sickness, mountains of pain—command those mountains to move in the Name of Jesus! You can heal the sick, raise the dead, cleanse the leper, and cast out demons with the assurance that greater is He who is in you than he who is in the world!

It's time to rise up and stand out. It's time to shine and show Jesus. To speak truth as you stand upon the firm foundation of absolute truth beneath your feet. To rise up on wings like eagles, never growing weary, and never fainting. You can choose to leave your worry at the foot of the cross as you walk in trust and fearless obedience fixing your eyes on Jesus, the author and perfecter of faith.

JESUS, YOU'RE BEAUTIFUL

I'm not exactly sure what it was about Jesus that drew people to Him but I don't think it had anything to do with His appearance. Scripture tells us He had no beauty or majesty to attract us to Him (see Isa. 53:2). Yet I feel the same pull. I feel the same deep need to run to Him, to fall at His feet, to wash His feet with my tears. To wipe His feet with my hair. To bring before Him my finest things and lay them at the very place that man would deem ugly. I am drawn to Him, to the beauty of His countenance, to the splendor of His presence. I can't help myself…*He's so beautiful to me.* His mercy, His grace, His *Name, Jesus.* Yeshua. Messiah. Savior. Friend. If I close my eyes, I can see His face. I can see His eyes. They are fierce yet filled with the deepest compassion I've ever known. It's His eyes, that intense sparkle of compassion that I see when I look in His eyes that causes me to declare,

Jesus, You're beautiful.

What glory it brings to the Father when we honor His Son. When we grasp the vastness of the separation the Father experienced for those 33 years Jesus was on the earth. The pain He must have felt. I miss my kids when they are at school or when they spend the weekend at their grandparents' house. I can't imagine our eternal Father ripping from the very center of His heart His beloved Son. Sending Him to the earth outside of His glory. Away from His eternal presence.

What a gift that the Father gave up His Son for that period of time so that you and I would never have to experience the agony of separation from God. Not ever. Once we realize what is available to us why would we ever walk away? *Do you realize?* Has the veil been lifted from your eyes, friend? Can you see Jesus? *His beauty?* That sparkle of compassion in His eyes? Can you sense the presence of God right now? He's with you, friend…His arms are open wide and His heart is exposed. He wants to love you. He wants to throw His arms around you, holding you and never letting go.

I have loved you with an everlasting love; I have drawn you with unfailing kindness. —Jeremiah 31:3

This is the God who plants the promise in your spirit, "*I think you can do anything.*" It's time to believe Him as we move into the final chapter of this journey we've been on together. Believing God is the launching pad propelling you into your destiny. It's a wild adventure, but it's the most amazing path to be on. The one of the unknown. Life outside the boundaries of the possible. Arms stretching into the unknown realm of the impossible as you soar, feeling the breeze in your hair, resting in the promised land of God's heart. What are you going to do, friend, now that your belief in God has taken on a new measure? Created for the impossible means putting legs to your faith, wings to your courage, a voice to your boldness, and arms to your compassion. Are you ready to *do something*?

What is He saying to you?

Chapter 14

JUST DO SOMETHING

*Therefore, since we are surrounded by such a huge
crowd of witnesses to the life of faith, let us strip
off every weight that slows us down, especially
the sin that so easily trips us up. And let us run
with endurance the race God has set before us.*
—HEBREWS 12:1 NLT

In 2008 just after my grandma passed away, I used to go sit at her grave and remember her. I would bring my journal with me and play worship music and write and think about the life she lived and the memories we shared. She had become such an important person in my life. She and I spent just about every day together in some capacity. We would watch movies together, grocery shop together, eat dinner together, play Yatzee together, and so much more. I didn't have kids at the time so I would stay at her house until the wee hours of the morning some nights. We would just sit up talking and laughing. She had become one of my very best friends.

When she passed away it was so sudden. The shock to my system was paralyzing at times. I had never experienced that kind of loss before. I didn't quite know what to do with myself. I knew she was with the Lord, but I just missed her so much.

There was something about her death that seemed to jolt life back into my system though. As I thought about her I found myself remembering the dreams of my youth. The books I would write. The places I would go. There was this resurgence of life flowing through me. I would go sit at her grave and pray, talk to God, and write in my journal. It was in these moments that I decided—*I'm going to go for it*. I'm going to write my book. The book that Jesus showed me when I was 17—I knew in my heart, nearly a decade later, that *it was time*. I didn't know how or where to even begin but that didn't matter, I knew God would guide my steps. In that moment I made a decision in my heart that even though I didn't know exactly what to do—I would trust the Lord. I yielded my will to God. I surrendered in a way that began to reignite His purpose in my weary soul. I went to the store, bought a nice leather-bound gold-trimmed journal, and just started writing.

It was three years later, just after the birth of my second child that I could feel my book swelling up in my spirit again. I could sense God was reminding me of the book that was in me, could sense being formed and developed just as my children had been. I sensed that one day very soon this promise would be birthed as well. All the while I continued to trust the Lord.

In the first few months of my son's life the voice of God became louder and louder. "*Just do something*," He would say, as if it were *that* simple. At this point God began wooing me with His promise. One day I opened up a magazine I received in the mail every month but had never read before. I flipped to the back page with purpose, as though I knew what I was looking for and there I read an article about a woman who had just written her second book and was sharing about her journey and how she started writing. Turns out she was a Christian and her story sounded much like mine. She had no idea how and where to begin but through a series of events she kept hearing, *just sit down and start writing...if not now, when?*

It sounds so simple, right?

Well friend, I can personally testify—it really is! Scary *yes*, but also: *simple*. It's called faith. Our job isn't to worry about outcomes; it's to be obedient. God wants us to simply trust Him. He's the author of our story. He will guide our every step if we will just make the choice in our heart to obey. *Nevertheless not my will, but your will be done, Lord.*

The Holy Spirit breaks our journey down into seemingly simple faith steps. Our path consists of trust, obedience, faith, and love. Our love compels us, our faith propels us, our trust sustains us, and our obedience keeps us moving forward in the will of God.

Do something...

Sit down and start writing...

So that's what I did. I did something. Nearly five years ago I sat down at my kitchen table during naptime and started writing what turned out to be the first blog post to what is now a ministry. What I wrote wasn't anything fancy. It was short and to the point. But it was an act of obedience. And the next thing I knew I was on a wild adventure with the Lord as He began fulfilling promise after promise after promise, one step at a time.

Just do something...

Created for the impossible means trusting God even when things don't seem to make sense. It means being willing to do *something* even when no road map is given.

OVERCOMING DISCOURAGEMENT

What has God promised you, friend? Oftentimes, we interpret God's promise to look a certain way and then find ourselves discouraged when we don't see Him bringing the promise to fulfillment the way we thought He would. Have you reinterpreted His promise? Ask the Holy Spirit to remind you of God's promise for your life. Write it down. And cling to it. Don't add to it or take away from it. Put down your red editing pen and choose to trust the Word of the Lord.

As a young person, I was filled with zeal for the Lord, ready to change the world and shake history. God had set a fire inside of me that I longed to share with the lost and hurting world around me. I was filled to the brim with vision and promise for my life. God was always speaking and I was quick to listen to Him. I truly felt unstoppable.

Something happened to my passion for God though as the years passed and the path God led me down looked *different* than I imagined it would. I couldn't understand why, in my mid-20s, I hadn't seen God fulfill some of the promises He had made to me nearly a decade prior. Eventually I allowed discouragement to settle in and before I knew it I was trading in my God-sized dreams for things I felt I could accomplish in my own strength. As I mentioned earlier in this book, the enemy was persistent with the narrative he was speaking over me,

You were never going to be a history maker that was just a song you used to sing…

World changer? Ha! You're just one small person in a great big world…

God was never going to fulfill that promise. See…You're nearly 30… it's too late!

And so on. He was nothing if not consistent. Sowing seeds of doubt, fear, condemnation, and despair. *Did God really say?* The sad thing is eventually I started to believe him. I began to let go of what God had promised…I began to wear discouragement as a heavy cloak around my shoulders. I minimized just about every promise God had made throughout my life until each one was small enough to fit inside the box I had labeled *"Unanswered Prayers"* to sit atop the shelf of disappointment.

But then something began to shift after I lost my grandma; God began replacing my pain with His promise. Then when I found out I was going to have a baby I could feel God begin to stir up hope, faith, and trust deep within me, setting me on a journey of renewed vision and fulfilled promises!

HIS-STORY MAKER

What is your story? How has God intercepted your path with His grace? Your story can shake history, friend. You have a testimony of Jesus in your life—what He has brought you through, kept you from, and rescued you from. Think about it for a moment. Your story can change the world! As you share your testimony, one by one, in your everyday life, you impact hearts. And then the people whose lives are changed share their story. The good news of Jesus spreads far and wide all because you dared to share your story with the *one* before you. Just as the men and women in the Bible never knew the impact their stories would have all these years later, so you may never know the impact of your story. But it's important you steward your testimony well by not hiding it under a bushel.

If you feel as though you're waiting for that *big thing* to happen—take a look around at what God has already done in your life! Fix your eyes on Jesus—the author and finisher of faith! He shows us how it's done. Friend, you make history everyday with your life! By remaining in Him and bearing fruit you live your life connected to the vine! You represent Jesus. It's His-story and He invites us in.

Created for the impossible means trusting that as a child of God your story is woven into *His*-story with beautiful crimson thread. Being one with Christ, you are truly His hands and feet in the earth in your everyday life.

Take a look at the life of Jesus. He wasn't doing anything flashy. He walked with His disciples. Spending time with them, He spoke life and truth into them. He encouraged them. He corrected them.

He wasn't self-seeking. He was about His Father's business, binding up the brokenhearted and setting the captives free. Healing the sick, raising the dead, loving the unlovely, driving out demons, showing kindness to the outcast. The woman at the well. The woman caught in adultery. Lazarus. The woman with the issue of blood. The *big things* were intertwined in His everyday life as He trusted His Father.

Friend, let's stop worrying about all the *big* things we want to *do* or the person we want to "*become.*" Instead, let's rejoice that we are part of *His*-story and we make history every day when we simply remain in Him and utilize the access Jesus died for us to have in fellowship with the Father. Everything we *do* for God is fruit of the relationship we have with Him. Dive deep into the secret place and rise up bold and courageous bearing fruit, rejoicing that your name is written in the Lamb's Book of Life.

This reminds me of the time the disciples returned from a journey and they were raving to Jesus about the outcome of their voyage.

> *The seventy-two returned with joy and said, "Lord, even the demons submit to us in your name."*
> *He replied, "I saw Satan fall like lightning from heaven. I have given you authority to trample on snakes and scorpions and to overcome all the power of the enemy; nothing will harm you. However, do not rejoice that the spirits submit to you, but* **rejoice that your names are written in heaven.**" —Luke 10:17-20

In other words, keep the main thing the main thing—of course the demons submit, they have no power or authority—I've given *you* the authority in my Name. The big deal here is that your names are written in Heaven. Rejoice that you're in the book. You're part of *My story.*

It's easy for us to get so caught up in what everyone else is doing and saying that we take our eyes off of Jesus and put them on man. We fall into comparison. We worry about our story looking so much different than their story. And we worry that somehow we have *missed it*. Friend, who wrote your story anyway? Let's stop trying to write ourselves into someone else's narrative and begin joyfully living the one God wrote just for us!

THERE'S A LONGING IN HIS HEART

There's a longing within the heart of God for people's eyes to be opened—for the blind to see, for the dead to rise, for those in captivity to be set free. The way has been paved. Now it's up to us as the hands and feet of Jesus to *go* into all the world, the world around us and the world afar, wherever God is calling us, to share the good news of the Kingdom with others.

Can you imagine how gut wrenching it must have been for Jesus to be here among people knowing the lengths the Father went to send His Son and the depths of His love for them, yet they rejected the truth? They had the Truth before them and they despised Him. They mocked Him. They weren't just rejecting the Son, but the Father— the One whom they professed to serve. Here stands Jesus—the way, the truth and the life saying if you only *knew* who it was who was speaking to you! If you only *knew* who it was standing before you... *Can you not see?*

> *Very truly I tell you, whoever accepts anyone I send accepts me; and whoever accepts me accepts the one who sent me.*
> —John 13:20

Jesus is longing that we have a shift in our perspective. He longs that the eyes of our heart open up and we awaken to the reality of His presence, the reality of who He is and what He means to the world.

In the story of Lazarus, Jesus had promised that his sickness would not end in death yet they couldn't *hear* what He was saying. They didn't understand. When He approached the home of Mary and Martha and found them weeping over their brother who had been dead for four days, He was moved to deep sorrow in His spirit. He longed for them to understand the truth, Jesus said to Martha,

> *I am the resurrection and the life. The one who believes in me will live, even though they die; and whoever lives by believing in me will never die. Do you believe this?* —John 11:25-26

Yet even after declaring this, Jesus wept with Mary who ran to Him, distraught over her brother's apparent death. I can only imagine the anguish in His heart for her, *"If you only knew! Why do you weep over this man? I've already promised he won't die…he is only sleeping. Shift your perspective! Look at Me. I Am the resurrection and the life. I Am Him. I Am here. Open your eyes."*

I believe that same longing exists today within the heart of the Lamb. The One who was slain. Looking out over all the earth. Seeing all the lost and the broken among us. Seeing the hopelessness in our hearts. I can just hear His heart crying out over all the world as He intercedes for us at the right hand of God, *"If you only knew what I did for you! If you only knew the lengths My Father went to bring Me to you! You're not alone, I Am with you! You have hope…you have Me. I love you! Open your eyes!"*

We've got to tell people about Jesus, friend. He's counting on us.

CREATED TO *KNOW* HIM

God created us to *know* Him. He's not some God seated on His throne dictating life. He's on His throne welcoming all to come near and sit at His feet. The invitation to come near was released through His Son, the Word made flesh, and sealed by His blood. God invites us all to come to Him. He says to all who are weary, *come to Me and you will find rest for your soul.*

Created for the impossible means *knowing* God, not just knowing *of* Him. It means we seek Him so that we can *find* Him! You can *know* God and you were created to know Him.

Are you convinced? Are you convinced that He loves you and cares about every detail of your life? That He made a way for you? That He created you to bear the fruit of His nature as you remain in Him? That God thinks you can do anything! Are you persuaded yet, friend? Then let's do this…let's rise up in boldness, meek as a lamb and bold as a lion! Shining the light of Christ to the lost and dying world around us in our everyday life! Let's *do something*. Modeling Jesus in our attitudes. Daily dying and daily leaving our old nature at the foot of the cross, putting on our new nature in the attitude of Christ as He washes us in His blood, revives us with His Word, and refreshes us with living water.

The river is rising, friend…

The time is now…if not now, *when?*

Say yes to God today. Don't wait for tomorrow, the day of Lord is now, today. The Kingdom of God is here. He has fresh bread for you today! The bread of life to distribute to all who are hungry…*He is more than enough.*

Now Go!

Then Jesus came to them and said, "All authority in heaven and on earth has been given to Me. Therefore go and make disciples of all nations, baptizing them in the name of the Father, and of the Son, and of the Holy Spirit, and teaching them to obey all that I have commanded you. And surely I am with you always, to the very end of the age."
—Matthew 28:18-20

Oftentimes we are overwhelmed at all the work that needs to be done. Jesus said, "The harvest is plenty but the laborers are few" (see Matt. 9:37). He is looking for a faithful few who will be His hands and feet (see 1 Cor. 12:27). He is looking for those who will dare to dream with Him.

Those who, having obtained an eternal perspective can see how each life matters in *His*-story. People who will be brave and walk in fearless obedience to step out of the boat, lock eyes with Jesus and trust Him—courageously running the race marked out for them.

For those who will lay aside their own selfish gain and ambition and determine in their heart that they will spend time in the secret place seeking the Father's heart. He's looking for those who aren't afraid to challenge culture with the truth. People who overflow in the joy of the Lord and are thus strong and courageous ambassadors for Christ, reflecting His glory to a dark and dying world. He's looking for those who will trust Him, step out of the boat and simply *do something.*

What have you heard from God? What has He called you to do? What dreams has He planted in your heart? What talents has He given you? Don't live in discouragement over what you feel God is *not* doing in your life, cling to His promise! Ask the Holy Spirit to show you what the next step is. Is it waiting on God? Is it trusting Him and leaning not on your own understanding? Is there something small He's been asking you to do but you've hesitated because it didn't seem big enough?

There is no small step of faith, friend. Every step into the unknown is a massive step of faith. So go for it! *Do something.* Love your neighbor. Teach your children. Serve your spouse. Help your church. Be a friend. Ask Jesus to give you divine appointments in your day. Steward your time well. Write a song. Speak a word. Share your story. Feed the hungry. Heal the sick. Raise the dead. Be present for your family. Help a stranger. Be kind. *Listen* to the voice of God and respond. Don't wait for tomorrow to make an impact when you could be making one in the lives of others right now, today.

So much of what Jesus did was spontaneous, yet with intense focus. Jesus was on His way to heal the 12-year-old girl who was dying when a woman touched His robe. He stopped. He had to find her. Meanwhile the little girl died, but Jesus later raised her to life. The physical miracles weren't the only miracles taking place. The miracle was also Jesus being able to maintain in His flesh—in His own humanity—humility, grace, and peace while thousands pressed on Him and pulled on Him. He was so sensitive to the Father and Holy Spirit. He was able to feel as power left His body prompting Him to stop and turn to the one, affirming her. Creating a moment in *His*-story for her story to be recorded and remembered, making an eternal impact.

Jesus shows us how to live, friend! He shows us how to balance the demands of life. He shows us how to prioritize. Through His intimate fellowship with the Father He was able to keep His mission in check, remaining in the Father's will. It wasn't about the large crowds; it was about who and what was before Him moment by moment ,day by day.

Do something…

Jesus did.

He listened to the Father and obeyed. One day at a time.

Writing this book was my time; now it is your time. You were divinely called to read these words and now your most loving Lord says it is your turn. It matters not where or how but only when. He will provide the resources you just need to provide the invitation! It's now your time!

Do something…

Created for the impossible isn't just the mountains He'll cause you to move or the seas He'll have you part, it's the fruit He'll cause you to bear. It's you making the choice day in and day out to remain in Him. It's you choosing life each and every day. It's you loving the unlovable. It's you loving yourself. It's you choosing to live for God and allowing God to live through you.

Created for the impossible is *you* believing what God says about you, yielding your life as a tool ready to be used by God in whatever way He sees fit. *Your will be done, Lord, and not my own.* It's you embracing the story you've been written into and lifting your head to lock eyes with Jesus who extends His hand to you, ready to walk with you. It's a merging of stories, yours and His, where now suddenly you begin to see that you've been making *His*-story all along.

What is He saying to you?

EPILOGUE

Dear Friend,

Thank you for taking time to incorporate this book into your life! I hope you were able to identify hindering thoughts, exchange them for what God says about you, and watch as God moved in your life!

Do you have a testimony to share? I would be honored if you would email me and share your story! Did you rededicate your life to the Lord? Or did you come to Christ for the first time? Please share! I would love to celebrate the victories in your life *with* you!

Do you have a prayer request? It would be my joy to pray with you. You're not alone!

> *God, I pray you stir up faith, hope, love, and courage within the hearts of each and every reader. That your presence would fill the space they are in right now. Guide their steps, transform their life, and restore anything that's broken in the mighty Name of Jesus! Amen.*

This book was written with all my heart and all my love—just for *you*! Dare to dream with God, friend. You were divinely created for the impossible for such a time as this! God thinks you can do anything!

I love you,

Krissy

krissy@notaloneministries.com

ABOUT KRISSY NELSON

Krissy Nelson is a mom, wife, author, speaker, and founder of Not Alone Ministries. She has a vision to help people see themselves the way God sees them. Her passion is being a light in the dark and voice of truth to a generation. She regularly hosts women's conferences and ministers at outreaches around the nation. Krissy is based in Pensacola, FL, with her husband and two children. For resources or booking information, visit her website at krissynelson.com.